HOW TO HUG A PORCUPINE

NEGOTIATING THE PRICKLY POINTS OF THE TWEEN YEARS

JULIE A. ROSS, M.A.

New York   Chicago   San Francisco   Lisbon   London   Madrid   Mexico City
Milan   New Delhi   San Juan   Seoul   Singapore   Sydney   Toronto

The **McGraw·Hill** Companies

Library of Congress Cataloging-in-Publication Data

Ross, Julie A., 1959–
    How to hug a porcupine : negotiating the prickly points of the tween years /
Julie A. Ross.
        p.   cm.
    Includes bibliographical references and index.
    ISBN-13: 978-0-07-154589-1 (alk. paper)
    ISBN-10: 0-07-154589-1
    1. Preteens.   2. Parent and child.   3. Child rearing.   I. Title.

    HQ777.15.R675   2008
    649'.124—dc22   2007052925

6 7 8 9 10 11 12 13 14 15 16 17 18 19 DOC/DOC 1 9 8 7 6 5 4 3 2 1 0

ISBN 978-0-07-154589-1
MHID   0-07-154589-1

Interior illustrations by Yali Lin

McGraw-Hill books are available at special quantity discounts to use as premiums and sales
promotions or for use in corporate training programs. To contact a representative, please visit the
Contact Us pages at www.mhprofessional.com.

This book is printed on acid-free paper.

Steve, you are my soul mate.
Thanks for sharing the adventures of parenting with me.
You are a brilliant writer and artist, and you always inspire
me to do my best work.

Emilie and Daniel, this is also for you,
for teaching me what I need to know
as a parent and as a person.

Contents

Acknowledgments

I want to thank my agent, Karen Gantz, who introduced herself to me after one of my lectures and began what has become a terrific and fruitful relationship. Her directness, enthusiasm, energy, and hard work helped get this book off the ground. I couldn't ask for a better literary agent, and I look forward to continuing to work together.

I also want to thank my editor at McGraw-Hill, Sarah Pelz. Sarah, your enthusiasm and bubbly spirit are contagious and are infused throughout this book. Thank you for always making me feel that this book was the highest priority in your day. Your corrections were brilliant, and I hope that I'll have the honor of working with you again someday in the near future.

I would be remiss if I didn't also thank all of the parents with whom I work, both privately and in ongoing groups. Their openness to learning new things, their deep compassion and love for their children, and their willingness to work hard at being the best parents they can be are inspirational to me. I'm eternally grateful for their willingness to share their stories, their successes, and their failures. Their contributions compose the bulk of this book.

Many thanks to my "readers"—Steve Ross, Kim Yerly, Wallace Anderson—for their honest opinions and feedback during the writing of this book. Thanks to my family, near and far, for brainstorming and sharing thoughts, quotes, and ideas with me. Thanks to my daughter, Emilie, for being my most enthusiastic cheerleader, and to my son, Daniel, for his expert grammatical advice.

Thanks to my terrific office assistants, past and present: April Glassey and Sonia Tarbill. I couldn't have done this without you guys—thanks for keeping everything else organized so I could take the time to write!

Finally, many thanks to Olivia Wiles, a middle schooler who came up with most of the chapter titles, for lending her authentic voice to this work.

➤ Introduction

In her timeless account of growing up, *Miss American Pie*, Margaret Sartor says that she began writing her diary in "the commonly acknowledged worst year of life, the seventh grade."

Seventh grade, part of the "tween" years and smack in the heart of middle school, is remembered by most of us in exactly the same way. That year epitomizes the middle schooler's reality: confusing, awkward, tough, and very, very uncomfortable. No small wonder, then, that our child's personality during these years resembles the often misunderstood porcupine. What looks like soft, cuddly fur is actually a strategic defense system, locked and loaded. That's why, one morning when your own little porcupine is happily humming a song from "The Little Mermaid" while putting her dishes in the sink, you can wind up with a face full of quills just because you asked her to take her shoes to her room. Or, on Friday you may end up consoling her for an hour when she's weeping because she has no friends, yet on Saturday she's made plans to go to the mall and hang out with six girls from school.

It's enough to make your head spin! Yet this is the very reason I love this age. I'm like a sailor drawn time and again to the high seas: I find the pitch and yaw of middle schoolers exhilarating. When they're excited, they are totally and completely committed to that excitement. When they are angry, they are unreservedly committed to that anger. They're equally silly and serious, childlike yet mature beyond their years.

Are they exhausting? They can be. Are they maddening? Sometimes. Are they intense and sometimes just plain loony? Yes! Can they be difficult to parent? You betcha.

As confused as our middle schooler may be, it's not unusual for us, as parents, to feel even more confused. After all, over the course of ten or eleven years, we've settled into a routine with our child. We've grown used to his habits, strengths, weaknesses, and energy level. We're familiar with the ways we need to talk to get him to do the things we want him to do. But then, sometime in the second decade of his life, he changes. Unexpectedly, the way we've done things for an entire decade doesn't work—and worse, our behavior or communication sometimes has unanticipated and unpleasant results. Out of the blue, we find ourselves with an entirely new creature—the middle schooler—but we have no idea what on earth to do with him or how to get through these challenging years.

Yet how we approach the middle school years is critical to our child's development. How we guide, teach, discipline, and engage with our tween determines how well he will do once full-blown adolescence hits. When he's a teenager, will he come home at midnight as we asked, or will we be looking for him on the streets at 3:00 A.M.? Will he talk to us about getting a tattoo, or just go out and get one? Will he listen to our values about drugs and sex, or will he slam his bedroom door and turn up the volume on his iPod so he can't hear us at all?

Middle school is our opportunity to successfully launch our tween into the adolescent years. Think about it this way:

Imagine that you are poised in a field, holding a bow and arrow. Ninety meters in front of you is a target with six concentric circles. Your eyes are on the target. Slowly, you pull the arrow back toward your shoulder and take careful aim. The tension in the bowstring builds: the right moment has come. You loose the arrow and watch it fly, holding your breath in anticipation.

Will the arrow hit the target? Will it be a bull's-eye? It depends, of course. If you've never practiced archery, then probably not. If you're a skilled archer, and you know how to aim and you've practiced for years, then you'll definitely hit the target, and you might even get a bull's-eye.

Being a parent is not unlike being an archer. We loose the arrow when our children enter high school, and whether the arrow hits the target depends in large part on how well we've aimed that arrow during the middle school years. But aiming the arrow during these years is not so easy. In fact, it's a little like learning to be an archer while an earthquake is going on!

That's why you need techniques: ones that allow you not only to circumvent your porcupine's defense system but also to pad yourself so that your own little porcupine's quills don't hurt so much.

And what's the point (no pun intended!), you might ask? Why not just shield our faces and plow through the tween years? I mean, won't adolescence be miserable no matter what we do?

The answer, believe it or not, is no! With the right tools and a little practice, adolescence can be a fulfilling and exciting time for parents and teens. To make it so, however, we must take advantage of the middle school years and use them as an opportunity to seek answers together with our child, not fight about what the answers are. We have to figure out how to sort through the confusion together, rather than agonize about it separately. Most important, we have to use these years to strengthen our relationship with our middle schooler and get to know who she's becoming so we can better guide her—now and in high school.

To do this, imagine that you were going to build a house. What would you need? You would need a specific set of tools for house building: a hammer, a saw, screwdrivers, nails, and so forth. It wouldn't be enough to simply understand philosophically what a house looks like, or that it needs plumbing and electricity and a good foundation. Philosophy won't build a house. The same is true of parenting a middle school child. It's not enough to have a set of philosophies. You also need a toolbox: a set of practical skills that specifically addresses the habits, needs, and concerns of the middle school child. These tools will allow you to effectively address your tween's attitude and values.

They will equip you to handle the inevitable power struggles, and to communicate your thoughts and advice about homework, friends, independence, and sexual development. And they will pad you so that you don't get stuck full of quills as you do so.

In the pages of this book, you will find the toolbox you need. You will hear the "voices" of the parents whom I've come to know over the years, both those within my private practice and those who attend the numerous parenting groups that I run. They are people just like you, because they come from all over our country and run the gamut of backgrounds, nationalities, and family configurations. You'll hear their children's voices as well, and you'll see examples of how the parenting skills that you'll be learning work in real life.

Down-to-earth, parent-tested strategies are present in every chapter, with detailed explanations of how and why they work. And they do work, as you will see from the real-life stories throughout.

Use this book as a practical guide—learn the strategies and fill your toolbox with tools that will allow you to hug your own porcupine. Not only will you find that the middle school years are more pleasant, but also you'll build the kind of relationship with your child that will make your friends envious once your child reaches the high school years.

The middle school years may be confusing, but they needn't be torturous. In fact, if we take the time to master a few basic skills, we might even find that these years, as well as the ones beyond, are downright pleasant.

1

Middle Schoolers: Hormonal, Disorganized, and Defiant

Sue is an even-tempered, thoughtful, and respectful parent. Her daughter, Maggie, has always been responsible, cooperative, and kind—a clear product of her mother's measured and educated approach to parenting. Imagine the shock when Sue arrives at our parents' group shortly after Maggie's thirteenth birthday and angrily blurts out, "Maggie is such a jerk!" My eyes widen, and collectively our jaws drop. There is stunned silence for a moment; then someone laughs, someone else applauds, and a chorus of comments begins: "It's so true!" "They're terrible!" "Thank you for saying it out loud!"

Middle schoolers can be infuriating! And while it's true that they're not all alike, one thing is certain: they aren't the children we knew during their elementary school years.

HAIRY AND HORRIBLE HORMONES

At some point during middle school, the body starts to produce the hormones necessary for our children to develop into adults (this generally occurs between the ages of ten and twelve for girls, and eleven and thirteen for boys). As parents, we will begin to see the outward, visible changes: pubic or body hair, body odor, breasts and a widening of hips for girls and, for boys, a broadening in the chest and a deepening of the voice, among other things. But, before these physical signs appear, there are inward changes, ones that can make our boys and girls alike feel extremely uncomfortable and can cause mood and energy swings, as well as psychological and physical discomfort.

It's these unseen changes that often give rise to the most frustration for parents. Because there's no direct, outward, concrete relationship between the inner and outer state, it can seem as though our children's behavior is coming out of the blue. If only a red light would appear in the middle of their foreheads, signaling "Hormone alert: shift occurring in 5, 4, 3, 2, 1" accompanied by beeping like a truck backing up, we could brace ourselves. Then, when Emily snarls and slams the door in our face, or when Jimmy loses his homework somewhere between his desk and his backpack, it would seem so much more understandable. We could say to ourselves, "Ah, yes, I saw the red warning light: this is a result of the changes he's going through." Unfortunately, no such warning system exists.

Life in Flux: Living on a Fault Line

Susan certainly discovered the lack of warning when Maggie turned into "a jerk." She expounds:

"I was in the kitchen, making a pot of tea, when Maggie came home from school. She had a bounce in her step, and I asked her, 'How was your day?' 'Great!' she said. 'It was awesome!' I gave her a cup of tea, and we started having this terrific conversation. She told me that she'd aced her bio test and that her Spanish teacher had complimented her on her accent. She hung out with her friends at lunch, and they'd made plans to go to the eighth-grade dance together. I was really enjoying our conversation! It went on like this for maybe twenty minutes, and then she seemed to be winding down, so I asked her if she had any homework. Well, I might just as well have lit the fuse to a bomb. She stood up, slammed her hand on the counter, and said, 'I can't believe you asked that. You never listen to me anymore, and you always ruin everything. I hate my life!' She ran out of the room and slammed the door to her bedroom, and she wouldn't talk to me for the rest of the night. Then, this morning, she acted as if nothing happened. I swear, I'm gonna kill her!"

Beep, beep, beep . . .
"Hormone alert: shift occurring in 5, 4, 3, 2 . . . "

Arrghh! Living with a middle schooler sometimes feels like living in an earthquake zone! Hmmm . . . actually, maybe that's the way we *should* view our lives during these years. If we imagine that we're living on a fault line—an area of the earth where seismologists know that earthquakes originate—then maybe we can be more prepared for upheavals. We may not be able to accurately predict when the earth will erupt underneath our feet, nor how much damage it will do, but at least we won't be altogether surprised when our preteens shift from nice to nasty.

By recognizing that earthquakes are a normal part of preadolescence and anticipating them, we can avoid the unpleasant feeling of surprise when they occur. This, in turn, will enable us to be more effective as parents by staying calm, not taking our child's remarks personally, and not overreacting. Because our children are in a state of flux, what they need most is for us to remain as stable as possible.

Anticipate earthquakes. Say to yourself:
"This is normal and to be expected."

Disorganized Doofus

"Kevin isn't having mood swings exactly," Abbie says after hearing about Susan's incident with Maggie. "It just that he's *so* disorganized! I got a note from his school saying he's missing *six* homework assignments in his English class. Well, I asked him about it, and he insisted that he had done all his homework and that his teacher must be mistaken. So, of course, I called the teacher, and—long story short—it turns out they were both right: he'd done his homework, but he hadn't turned it in! I found it in the bottom of his backpack! When I asked him why he didn't hand it in, he said the teacher never asked for it. That doesn't even make sense!"

It's so frustrating, isn't it? And the reality is that our middle schooler's "non-sense" represents a lot of what our children will do during these years. But while what they do may not make sense from an adult perspective, we need to remember that the preadolescent brain is very different from the adult brain. In fact, it's been described as a single-lane country road turning into a superhighway. If we envision our children's developing brains in just that way, as a construction site with backhoes and bulldozers, concrete mixers and dump trucks, it becomes easier to see why they might misplace their homework between the backpack and the teacher's desk. Disorganization is actually part of the illogic of preadolescence. Even kids who were organized prior to middle school can "lose it" during these years. Later, we'll discuss how both Susan and Abbie can use specific techniques to handle their preteens' behaviors, but for now what's important is to recognize that the internal changes our children are going through during these years require a different perspective on our part. Only if we make an internal shift in the way we see our child can we remain firm, steady, and strong—qualities that will help our children feel safe and secure in this tumultuous time.

Disorganization:
"This is normal and to be expected."

METAMORPHOSIS

"I guess what's hard for me," Carol says with tears in her eyes, "is that I feel as if I've lost touch with who Tracy is. It was just last year that I felt we had a superstrong relationship. Now that she's in middle school, she's . . . different. We're not close anymore, and I don't know what to do about it. She's so sensitive and touchy about everything. I can't even figure out what to say without making her mad or having her burst into tears. . . . I miss her."

During middle school, it can, indeed, feel as though we've "lost" our child. The changes appear to be so deep, so all-encompassing, that our child often seems to be someone we don't know, and maybe even someone we don't like very much.

But what feels like loss is really transformation. The essence of our children remains, but they are drawn inward for a period in order to develop properly. Similar to the caterpillar who spins a chrysalis to protect itself while it changes into a butterfly, our children "protect" themselves with anger, sensitivity, tears, defiance, and disorganization. These behaviors are the human chrysalis, the outer shell that protects the delicate, unformed butterfly while it's at its most vulnerable.

As we support our children during this metamorphosis, we must remember that they are, essentially, "caterpillar soup"—neither caterpillar nor butterfly—and, just as with other members of the animal kingdom, this stage of metamorphosis is a delicate one.

Butterfly keepers know that during the chrysalis stage, the growing creature must be handled with care. Moving the chrysalis around too much, shaking it, or exposing it to extremes in temperature can damage the delicate process that the future butterfly is undergoing. We too must treat our charges with care during this transformation. We must measure our words in the way that butterfly keepers measure how much they handle a chrysalis. Likewise, we must protect our children from extremes in our emotional temperature so that their newly forming identity can begin to take shape and so that we will not damage our relationship with them during this time.

Treat the chrysalis with care.

All of this is not to suggest that we become permissive, soft parents. In fact, as you will see, setting limits remains an important part of keeping our children safe and helping them make good decisions. However, the way in which we set limits and guide and care for our children has to take into account the developmental changes that they are undergoing. In essence, we too must go through a metamorphosis.

THE LONG VIEW OF PARENTING

Looking ahead to the time when our children will be independent from us can help us decide how we can be the most effective during the middle school years. This requires asking ourselves not only, "Is what I'm doing working?" but also, "What am I teaching my child?" Think of it as taking the long view of parenting.

Up until now, our primary job has been to protect our child from the potential harm the world may inflict upon him and from the poor choices he may make. Thus, we've frequently judged our effectiveness as parents based on the direct, visible, and often immediate results that we can see. We gauge whether our parenting style "works" by watching for a change in our child's behavior.

Beginning now, we want to shift to a *preparatory* mind-set and ask ourselves, "How can I prepare my child to protect himself and make independent and appropriate choices that will benefit him in the future?" This shift isn't easy, because we will not necessarily be able to measure the effectiveness of our parenting by whether we see immediate and visible results. In addition, making the shift from protection to preparation requires that we be flexible, because during middle school, our child will still need a little bit of both.

THE RELATIONSHIP APPROACH

As we transition to a more proactive and long-range stance in our parenting, we want to shift our focus from controlling our child's behavior to building, strengthening, and fortifying our relationship with him. This has several benefits. First, it doesn't "jostle the chrysalis" and disrupt the developmental process that our child is undergoing. Second, it lays the foundation for the adolescent years, when we will no longer have control over our child.

Let me repeat that. In adolescence, we will no longer be able pick up our son and put him in his room as we did when he was a toddler. We will no longer be able to coerce our daughter or threaten her as we did when she was in elementary school. We won't be able to rely on physical force or to count on our son's regarding us with enough awe to be fearful of how we might punish him. In other words, we won't have direct control over our child when she reaches adolescence. This is shocking, but it's true. When our child becomes a teenager, we will have to rely *entirely* on whether our relationship with him is strong enough so that he is influenced by our needs, desires, and values.

Four primary qualities distinguish the relationship approach. They are respect, support, reciprocity, and collaboration. Further chapters will identify specific techniques we use to achieve each of these qualities in our relationship with our child. Let's start by seeing what each of them means.

The Quality of Respect

To appreciate the importance of engaging our middle schooler in respectful ways, it's helpful to understand the role that respect plays in a child's developing sense of self. In an article called "On Kids and Confidence," Dr. Stephen Garber and his associates describe the components of self-worth as taking the shape of a pyramid with four levels:

Peer Influence
Parental Feedback
Real Accomplishments
Unconditional Positive Regard

The bottom level of the pyramid, the foundation upon which all else rests, is what another distinguished psychologist, Dr. Carl Rogers, calls "unconditional positive regard." For us, as parents, this means the unconditional love and acceptance that we show to our children. Looking at the pyramid, we can see that the broader the base, the less weight peer influence will exert on our preteens. However, if we're stingy with our love and acceptance, if our middle schooler feels that he has to earn our love through what he accomplishes, then his sense of self-worth will be compromised. He'll never feel good about himself, no matter how much he achieves.

I'm sure you know people for whom this is true—adults who make enormous amounts of money and whose achievements are acknowledged by trophies and plaques and degrees. These are the people who claim, each year, that as soon as they achieve a certain level of financial security or recognition, they will retire so that they can "enjoy life." Yet, at the end of each year, they still don't feel satisfied with what they've accomplished or earned.

I believe this happens because satisfaction doesn't occur through achievement, but rather by being given what I consider to be every child's birthright: the free, unconditional love and acceptance of one's parents. Note that we start out well in this regard with our children. Think back to the first time you laid eyes on your child, the first time you held him in your arms. Do you remember that overwhelming feeling of love that poured out of you? Your child didn't have to do anything to earn your love; just the fact that he existed was enough for you to give your love to him freely and unconditionally.

Unfortunately, as our children begin to "do stuff," and as their achievements (or lack thereof) come under our scrutiny, we often begin to withdraw our "positive regard" and convey the impression that they need to earn our love. This happens especially in middle school, when our children's behavior may be shifting radically from day to day, when the words they use with us may be hurtful, and when we feel personally attacked by them.

It's during this tumultuous time when, because of their developing sense of self, they need more than ever to feel that they have stable and unconditional love from us. This period, in fact, is the most dangerous—and, unfortunately, the most common—time for us to slip into disrespectful communication or behavior.

We show unconditional love and acceptance and build the foundation of our children's self-worth when we communicate in respectful ways toward them, even when we're angry, frustrated, or bewildered at their behavior. But what, exactly, is respectful behavior?

Love and accept the "caterpillar soup."

Respectful Behavior. We're acting respectfully toward our middle schoolers, and building their sense of self-worth, when we can answer yes to any or all of the following questions:

- ◄ Would I treat my spouse or partner this way?
- ◄ Would I treat my best friend this way?
- ◄ Would I want to be treated this way?

As we ask ourselves these questions, we want to examine three different factors:

- ◄ Our words
- ◄ Our tone of voice
- ◄ Our body language

So, our questions might become:

- ◄ Would I use these words with my spouse?
- ◄ Would I use this tone of voice with my best friend?

◄ Would I want my child to use this body language/facial expression in speaking to me?

If we answer no to any of these, then we're "jostling the chrysalis" and interfering with the developing "butterfly."

The Paradox of Parenting. In my third book, *Now What Do I Do? A Guide to Parenting Elementary-Aged Children*, I wrote about what I call the "paradox of parenting," which is this: We love our children more than anything in the world; in fact, we love our children so much that if we were given the choice between losing a child and losing one of our own limbs, we would, without hesitation, say, "Take my arm. Take my leg. Don't touch my child." That's the depth of our love. Yet, even though we love our children more than anything in the world, there are times when we treat them in ways we wouldn't treat a stranger on the street. What a shame. They are our most important gift. And during the time when they are struggling to develop into the butterfly they will become, they need more than ever to have our respect and to be shown that they are unconditionally loved.

The Quality of Support

Support is another quality of the relationship approach, and it comes directly out of a sense of respect for our child's developmental needs during middle school.

During this time, our children are beginning to feel the pull from specific developmental needs that will eventually define both their adolescence and their adulthood. They are:

◄ To become independent from us
◄ To prove that they're different from us

These developmental urges can be confusing and upsetting for middle schoolers, because children of this age are also keenly aware that they are still dependent on us to have their most fundamental needs met: housing, money, food, and so forth. They are also highly aware that they will not be out from under our jurisdiction for another five to seven years. This amount of time is an eternity to a middle schooler—after all, it equals a third of the child's life! Having to wait an eternity before being fully independent can cause a child to feel trapped, helpless, and angry.

Supporting our middle schoolers during these years means recognizing that their burgeoning developmental needs are in direct conflict with their reality. It means giving them healthy and appropriate outlets for their needs. This is a vital component of parenting at this stage. If we fail to do this, it's the equivalent of holding a baby back from learning to walk. No one would ever consider doing such a thing. In fact, as our toddler learns to walk, we applaud, support, and encourage this new level of independence. This is the way it should be with our middle schoolers as well: while their developmental needs may be less visible than walking, they are no less critical to their growth and health as human beings.

Parvani's twelve-year-old daughter, Uma, asked to walk to her gymnastics class by herself. This was a big step, since Uma would have to cross several major streets in New York City, and Parvani felt nervous about agreeing. But she thought it over and decided that if Uma carried a cell phone and called her when she arrived at the gym, then she would feel safe. Uma agreed.

The first day that Uma traveled by herself, Parvani reminded her of the importance of calling once she arrived. Uma swore that she would. Parvani watched the clock to estimate Uma's arrival at the gym, and when she was sure a sufficient amount of time had passed for her to get there, there was still no phone call. Parvani went to the gym and found Uma happily chatting with her friends. Seeing her mother, she was immediately remorseful: "Mom! Oh, I'm *so* sorry. I'm *so* sorry. I totally forgot. I promise it won't happen again; I promise!" Parvani agreed to let her try again. The next week, the same situation arose, and Parvani once again found Uma chatting with her friends, having "forgotten" to call.

Truth to tell, Parvani was beginning to feel like a doormat! Here she is, trying to give Uma the independence she needs, and Uma is walking all over her, not calling and being totally irresponsible. Not only is this annoying, but it's frightening too, because Parvani has no idea if Uma has arrived safely.

This is a fairly classic case of middle schoolers' behavior when they're struggling to achieve independence. Despite the fact that Parvani is supporting Uma's developmental need for independence by allowing her freedom to go to gymnastics alone, Uma still feels restricted in some way—evidenced by the fact that she's "forgetting" to call. At this point, Parvani could clamp back down on Uma and take the independence away. However, there's a more effective, relationship-based way to handle it that will still get the results that Parvani wants and needs.

The Quality of Reciprocity

Healthy adult relationships are reciprocal, which means that there's a "give-and-take" quality to them. Sometimes one person's needs take precedence; sometimes the other person's needs take precedence. And often, compromise is required to achieve a "win-win" solution so that both people's needs are met. In the middle school years, this quality extends to the parent-child relationship as well.

Engaging the quality of reciprocity means answering two questions: What are my needs? What are my child's needs?

In Parvani and Uma's case, Parvani needs to know that Uma has arrived safely. Uma needs to feel independent from her mother. Let's take a look at a few more examples of reciprocity:

Preteen's behavior	Preteen's possible need	Parent's possible need(s)
Extensively calling or IMing friends	Connect with her peer group	Ensure that the phone bill doesn't get out of hand and/or that the preteen doesn't neglect her homework or chores
Not washing or bathing frequently enough	Exhibit different values from his parents	Have the preteen maintain proper hygiene

Preteen's behavior	Preteen's possible need	Parent's possible need(s)
Not doing homework	Prove she doesn't care about "that stuff" and is therefore different from her parents in that regard	Ensure that the preteen gets a good education
Playing music too loudly	Show he has different tastes in music from those of his parents	Limit noise in the house to a reasonable level

We can see by this short list that much of what the preteen does is an attempt to satisfy the developmental needs of independence and differentiation. For your middle schooler to continue to grow in a healthy direction, her needs must be met.

As a parent, you have a right for your needs to be met as well. This means, however, that you will have to get past the "Because I said so" paradigm and start to learn how to articulate what you really need from your middle schooler. Because your needs will likely be more varied than your middle schooler's, you'll also have to take the time to think before you speak so that you can express yourself clearly.

Once you grasp the concept that you and your preteen have reciprocal needs that must be identified in order to make your relationship and life together easier, it's time to look at the role that collaboration can play as you transition to a relationship approach with your child.

The Quality of Collaboration

The quality of collaboration in middle school allows all parties the possibility of having their specific, individual needs met. It reduces the chance of rebellion and defiance, keeps the middle schooler's developmental needs at the forefront of negotiations, and yet still allows parents to retain their authority and role as decision maker.

Collaboration means adopting a win-win philosophy. Rather than seeing the problems that arise with our middle schoolers as a series of battles to be won, we need to shift our thinking to encompass the possibility that there is a middle ground where both parties can feel satisfied. Neither may get exactly what he or she wants, but both will get what they need.

In Parvani and Uma's case, Parvani recognizes that Uma might feel embarrassed if she has to "call Mommy" when she arrives at the gym. She might "lose face" in front of her friends. Parvani can offer Uma "a way out" by suggesting that she send Uma a text message to which Uma can reply in a more anonymous way. This will allow Uma to touch base with her mother without having to speak to her on the phone in front of her friends.

Ultimately, collaboration is a dialogue during which we can either present what we think each individual's needs are or explore with our middle schooler what those needs might be. Later, we'll see how to use the technique of "cooperative communication" to engage our child in a dialogue to achieve a win-win result.

First, however, we must learn to "listen with heart."

LISTENING WITH HEART

In *The Little Prince*, by Antoine de Saint-Exupéry, the fox says, "It is only with the heart that one can see rightly; what is essential is invisible to the eye." To listen with heart means discarding our "critical eye" and opening our hearts to our middle schooler. Criticism and judgment will only blind us to our middle schooler's developmental needs, close our hearts, and make it impossible to listen.

How Important Is Listening?

In an article written for the *Utne Reader* called "Tell Me More," Brenda Euland said the following about listening: "When we are listened to, it creates us, makes us unfold and expand. Ideas actually begin to grow within us and come to life. . . . When we listen to people there is an alternating current, and this recharges us so that we never get tired of each other. We are constantly being re-created."

"Listening with heart" to our preteens means creating a magnetic and creative space so that they are drawn toward us instead of pushed away. It means that we will never get tired of each other and that we can constantly "re-create" our relationship with our burgeoning adolescent.

For me, as a mother, the ability to "re-create" my relationship with my children is a redemptive concept. I have made many mistakes and will make many more, but if I know that I can re-create my relationship with my children and redeem my mistakes through the process of listening, I can breathe a sigh of relief. I don't have to be perfect. Neither do you.

What Is Listening?

The best definition of listening that I've ever come across in my years as a parent educator comes from Stephen R. Covey's book *The Seven Habits of Highly Effective Families*: "Seek first to understand, then to be understood." Listening means trying to understand our preteens before we judge, lecture, advise, or otherwise speak to them about their behavior.

As difficult as it may seem to do this, we start out perfectly in this regard, as pointed out earlier. When our children are infants, we spend twenty-four hours a day seeking to understand them without trying to make ourselves understood. We are constantly asking ourselves: "What does my baby need? Does she need to be held, changed, fed, put to sleep? How can I meet her needs?"

Of course, it's easier to do this with infants, because it's clear that trying to make ourselves understood would be a useless endeavor. They don't speak; therefore, they can't understand. Also, because they don't speak, we're not focused on their words. Instead, we're paying attention to their behavior and listening to the tone of their crying. Through their behavior and tone, we're seeking to interpret and understand: Does she look as if she's in pain? Does that sound like his "hungry cry?"

Unfortunately, once our children begin using words, we often lose sight of the importance of behavior and tone of voice in the skill of listening and focus too much attention on the words our child is using.

Listening means paying more attention to
behavior and tone of voice than to words.

Interpret Their Behavior and Tone

Trying to understand our preteens means recognizing that with any negative behavior or language, it's likely that they are attempting to communicate a specific developmental need. It means paying attention to their behavior and tone, using the same skills of interpretation that we used when they were infants, and then applying them to this new developmental stage.

Let's see how Parvani does this with Uma. Although Parvani initially felt annoyed with Uma for "forgetting" to call on the second occasion, she gave herself some time to regain her perspective and attempted to discard her "critical eye." Remembering that she had to respect Uma's developmental needs, she said: "Uma, I'm sensing that even though Dad and I are allowing you to walk to gymnastics alone, it still may not feel like the amount of independence you need. Do you think that's accurate?"

Timing is as important as technique. Try to pick a
time to talk to your preteen when you're no longer
angry and you're both relaxed.

"No, Mom, really, I'm sorry. I forgot to call you again, I know; I'm sorry. I promise that I will next time."

"Wait, hon. You seem to think that I'm criticizing you for not calling."

"Well, yeah. Aren't you?"

Note that Parvani doesn't barge ahead with her agenda. Instead, she "listens" nicely to Uma and stops to reflect what she thinks might be Uma's interpretation of her words. She looks beneath the surface instead of taking Uma's apology at face value. This allows the communication to stay "clean" and "clear." Often, if we barge ahead, the waters begin to get muddied, and by the end of the conversation we may not have the outcome we were hoping for, simply because we didn't take the time to address individual feelings or misconceptions as they arose.

Parvani continues: "No, that's not what I was saying. I'm no longer mad about your not calling. It seems to me that there must be a reason you didn't call, and I'm just trying to understand that."

Parvani exhibits respect here by saying that she assumes Uma has a good reason for forgetting to call, rather than implying that Uma is simply being irresponsible. Preteens live up to our expectations, and if we communicate that they're irresponsible, they will become even more so. Remember that they're still learning responsible behavior, and they will make mistakes along the way.

You can look beneath your middle schooler's irresponsible behavior *without* being a doormat!

Uma replies: "No, there's no reason. I just forgot. I mean, I got to the gym, and my friends were there, and we just started talking, and then I forgot."

"Well, it sounds as if you have a great time with your friends and you're enjoying the independence. What about this: would it be easier if I called you?"

"Oh, Mom, that would be embarrassing," Uma groans.

"OK, well, how about this: I'll call you, and you won't pick up. But, you'll know that I called, and you can anonymously text me back, even just saying, 'Hi,' which will let me know that you arrived. That way, your friends won't have to know that it was me calling."

Uma brightens. "OK! That sounds good, Mom. Thanks!"

In this conversation, Parvani practices "listening with heart" well. She looks beneath Uma's seemingly irresponsible behavior and interprets what's going on. She utilizes the quality of collaboration in their relationship by assuming there's a win-win solution somewhere, and she proposes a solution that she feels will meet both of their needs.

Clearly, if Uma winds up not texting her mother back when they try this proposed solution, then it will be time to set some limits, the mechanics of which we will discuss later in the book.

What If Your Preteen Is Belligerent?

Obviously, Parvani's conversation with Uma was made easier by Uma's being receptive and open. It's much harder to "listen with heart" when our preteens are spewing venom. In fact, it's a little like trying to hug a porcupine. If its quills are down, everything is fine, but if its quills are erected, well, someone's going to get hurt, and it's not going to be the porcupine! If your preteen is in defensive mode, the best way to refrain from taking it personally is to walk away. Engaging with her now will only result in barbs coming at you.

Timing is everything!

When Helen, aged twelve, came home from school, Jennifer could tell that trouble had walked in the door. Helen slammed her books on the table and glared at her mother, saying, "You made a fool of me in school today!"

"What are you talking about?" Jennifer asks.

"You made me wear this jacket 'cause you said it was cold out. It wasn't cold, no one was wearing a jacket, and I looked like a total idiot. Don't you *ever* tell me what to wear again."

Jennifer's temper flares. "Excuse me," she retorts. "Don't *you* ever speak to me in that tone of voice again. You're an idiot if you live your life according to what your stupid friends think. When are you going to get a brain and start thinking for yourself?"

Oops! The problem here is that Jennifer is rising to the bait that Helen's offering, and in doing so, she's effectively transforming into a twelve-year-old herself. In addition, she's role-modeling the very behavior that she's asking Helen to eliminate. This is one of the most disastrous things we can do as a parent, for several reasons:

- ◀ Our children are much better at being preteens than we are. If we fight with our preteen as though we're also in middle school, rest assured that our preteen will win.
- ◀ Our preteens need for us to remain emotionally connected and stable, because they're so unstable during this period. They need to know that we may not love their behavior but that, despite the fact that they're uncomfortable during their metamorphosis, we aren't going anywhere, and we will continue to love them, confident that, in due time, they will get through this.

So, how do we maintain a sense of connection with a preteen who's pushing away, especially when her quills are raised and loving her actually hurts?

It's hard to hug a porcupine!

LOVE TICKETS

There is power in the written word. Time and again it's been proved that human beings are more likely to believe and remember what they read than what they hear. Writing a note that expresses our love or that commends our middle schooler for something we appreciate about him is an effective way to stay connected with him.

I call these notes "love tickets," the name for which was given to me by a four-year-old boy. Here's his story: Arturo's mother wrote him notes to take to school every day. Sometimes they'd simply say, "I love you"; sometimes they'd say, "I can't wait to see you after school"; other times they might say, "Pretend this is a hug from me!" One day, Arturo came home from school crying inconsolably. His mother scooped him up into her lap and hugged and rocked him until he calmed down. Then she asked, "Sweetheart, what happened? Did someone hurt you? Did you fall down or hurt yourself at school?" With tears still in his eyes, he blurted out, "No . . . I lost my love ticket."

"Love tickets" are a meaningful and powerful form of communication for children of all ages, but they work especially well with middle schoolers, for several reasons:

- People believe what they see in writing. Preteens are no different. When you write out your love to your middle schooler, he's more likely to believe *and remember* it than if you simply tell him orally.
- Because it's hard to hug a porcupine without getting stuck full of quills, love tickets allow us to love from a safe distance. If your preteen responds badly (although very few of them do), you aren't within striking range.
- Love tickets allow our preteens to absorb our messages in their own time. They have time to smooth their quills and let their own emotions settle down before allowing us to get close to them again.

Writing "Love Tickets"

Love tickets can take two forms: they can either express pure and unconditional love or encourage a specific positive behavior that your preteen exhibited. Here are some examples of each:

Specific positive behavior	Unconditional love
"I liked the song you were playing yesterday."	"I love you."
"Thanks for helping in the kitchen last night."	"I'm glad you're you."
"I enjoyed watching television with you last night."	"You're awesome."

There are a few guidelines that you should follow in writing "love tickets" to your middle schooler:

◄ **Short and simple is best.** The more flowery you become, the more likely children are to brush aside your encouragement. For example, "I love you even when we argue" is better than "I know we had an argument today, but I want you to know that I love you so much anyway because you're a terrific kid, and I know you're just going through a hard time. I want you to know that I understand what you're going through . . . blah, blah, blah (you get the picture)."

◄ **Stick to the present.** For example, don't say, "I miss our relationship." This implies that you're unhappy with the relationship in its current state, which, though it may be true, does not need to be articulated to your preteen.

◄ **Don't use your love tickets to criticize your teen, even subtly.** Don't say, "I love you, but I wish you wouldn't play your music so loudly." The word *but* negates everything that comes before it, making your love ticket worthless.

CAN YOU REALLY LOVE A PORCUPINE?

There's no doubt that you won't always *feel* loving toward your preteen, but that's OK; your child won't always feel loving toward you either! The key lies in continuing to *express* your love even if you don't feel that way. Love tickets make this easier, because they can be written when you do feel loving and given to your preteen when you don't. Some parents worry that they're "being phony" if they express love when they aren't feeling loving, but this is not true. If you've never felt loving toward your child, then saying you love him *would* be a lie. However, expressing your underlying love for him when you're angry at him isn't a lie—it's just good timing.

One final suggestion: write the love tickets on a regular basis. One or two a week would be nice. You'll be surprised at how they can strengthen your relationship when things are good and transform your relationship when things are tough.

Isabelle and her thirteen-year-old son, Mitchell, had been going through a particularly tough time. In fact, Mitchell hadn't spoken to her in several days except with grunts and shrugs. Often, he would closet himself in his room, chatting online with his friends while music blared. After weeks of his surly behavior, Isabelle was at her wit's end. I suggested she write him a love ticket, which she did: "Dear Mitchell, I know our relationship has been a little rocky. I just want you to know that I will always love you." She slipped it under his door and went into the kitchen to make dinner. About thirty minutes later, she heard Mitchell's bedroom door open. She continued with what she was doing and didn't look up when he entered the kitchen. He shifted from foot to foot for a moment in that slouchy way that preteens and teens have, and then he said, "So, um, do ya need any help?"

Love tickets are powerful. Used often, they strengthen the fabric of our relationship with our middle schooler so that it can withstand even the toughest times.

2

The Overwhelmed "Slacker"

The shift from elementary school to middle school represents an enormous leap in academic and social pressure for preteens. Coinciding directly with their developmental disorganization and their rapidly changing bodies, it can be overwhelming. This is sometimes difficult for us to understand, in part because the academic expectations for middle schoolers are vastly different today from when we were in middle school.

In her book *The Organized Student*, Donna Goldberg says that middle schoolers today "have substantially more work . . . [and] . . . overloaded schedules. . . . [They are] drowning in paper, inundated with handouts, printouts, and packets. They lose hours each day to e-mail, instant messaging, and the Internet."

In addition, academic pressure has increased in recent years. In *The Overachievers*, Alexandra Robbins describes a shift to what she calls "a high-stakes testing culture" beginning in 2002 when the No Child Left Behind Act was signed into law, requiring schools to test children on reading, math, and science every year beginning in the third grade. Schools feel pressured to produce children with high test scores to show that students are making "acceptable progress." This stress is passed along to the student body. Robbins says, "The exclusive emphasis on tests has left students sick with stress in even the youngest grades; some schools reported that on testing days, up to two dozen children vomit on their test booklets."

Think about what you may remember of your own middle school experience. Most of us shudder at the recollection: it was a challenging time, to be sure. However, upon reflection, it may look almost idyllic compared with what preteens face today. We had lockers and books; they have backpacks and loose papers. We had one or two extracurricular activities that we did mostly for fun; they may have up to half a dozen, and they're often expected to excel at all of them. We didn't think about the college admission process until high school; they're being pressured to set their sights on the Ivy League schools as early as sixth grade. It's no wonder that middle schoolers complain about feeling stressed!

A VICIOUS CYCLE

One by-product of this stressful environment is that it can overwhelm students who may not come by organizational skills naturally. Olivia complains about eleven-year-old Jordan: "Jordan's a slacker. He was lazy in elementary school, and now it's as if he's turning into a sloth. I'm really worried that he's going to fail!"

This, of course, is somewhat reminiscent of Kevin in Chapter 1, who did his homework but, because his teacher didn't ask for it, failed to turn it in. The difference, in the words of his mother, Abbie, is that "Kevin is devolving. He used to be pretty organized, and now it's as if he's turning into a lower life-form."

In truth, it's probably not laziness or devolution. Instead, it's far more likely that both middle schoolers are completely overwhelmed.

Many preteens become disorganized in middle school, no matter what they were like in their elementary school setting. Organization is not an instinctual skill for most people; it must be learned. The new and increased pressure of the middle school environment, combined with our child's lack of knowledge about organization, results in what I call the "overwhelmed slacker" phenomenon. Because the child doesn't instinctively understand how to stay organized, he gets behind. This makes him feel overwhelmed, which contributes to his lack of organization. It's a vicious cycle.

"But what am I supposed to do with that information?" Olivia exclaims angrily. "I'm furious with him. It's not that hard: you write down your assignments; you come home; you do the assignment. Do you realize that when I asked him one day if he'd done his homework, he said yes, and after he went to school, I found his entire binder, with the incomplete assignments, shoved under his bed? It's ridiculous!"

Exactly! How hard is it? It's completely bewildering when our children behave like this. It makes us feel as if we're losing our minds!

HANDLING YOUR OWN FEELINGS

However, our strong feelings can get in the way of being effective parents. Therefore, when we have negative feelings about our middle schooler, it's important to work with those feelings prior to launching into a technique. For example, most of the time, anger is masking other, more subtle feelings; if we can identify the feelings underneath our anger, we can be more productive. Why? Anger is such a powerful emotion that it can get in the way of helping our middle schooler succeed academically, which is our ultimate goal. In addition, it will shake the chrysalis and undermine our relationship with him.

Our anger "shakes the chrysalis."

Before we look at what feelings Olivia and Abbie might be having, I want to acknowledge that feelings are difficult to change. We can't magically snap our fingers and say, "OK, I'm not going to be angry anymore." However, feelings are part of a cycle within which there are two "windows of opportunity"—two chances to make a change that may influence our feelings. Because our anger is so threatening to a middle schooler, it's worthwhile taking a look at what Michael Popkin in his video series *Active Parenting Today* refers to as the "Think-Feel-Do Cycle."

The Think-Feel-Do Cycle

In our lives with our children, cycles are spontaneously triggered by everyday events. When a problem or emotionally charged event occurs, most people believe that we have feelings about that problem:

Event (problem)　　　　　　　　**Feelings**

However, the truth is that problems trigger specific *thoughts*, which *then* lead to feelings. Let's take a look at Olivia's problem and see how that works:

Event (problem)
Jordan hides homework
under bed

Olivia's thought
He'll never get into
high school!

Olivia's feeling
Anger
(masking fear)

Look at the word *never* in Olivia's thought. This is an example of what often happens: our thoughts tend toward the extreme and are thus inflammatory. In this case, Olivia's thought inflames her fear into anger.

In the think-feel-do cycle, our feelings cause us to react:

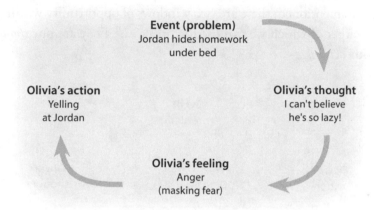

The action that we take as parents represents the next *event*, which then triggers a cycle for our middle schooler:

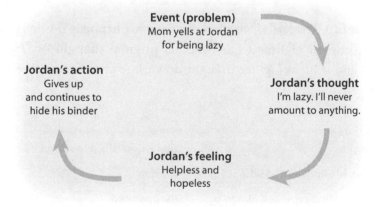

In this example, you can see how cycle upon cycle could be triggered, perpetuating the very problem that Olivia would like to see remedied.

Breaking into the Cycle

So, what do we do about these cycles? Well, if we assume that we have to change our feelings, we face a daunting task. Anyone who's ever been in the grip of a strong emotion such as rage or envy can tell you that it's impossible to simply choose not to feel that way. Fortunately, as mentioned, there are two windows of opportunity within the cycle, either of which we can use to "break in." They are our *thoughts* and our *actions*.

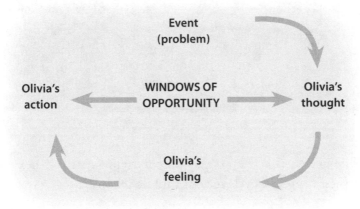

The First "Window": Thought. Let's see what happens if Olivia takes just a little bit of time to analyze her original thought of "He's so lazy!" and if breaking her thought down into specifics changes how she feels:

Thought	Olivia's possible feelings
"Jordan will flunk out of school."	Afraid
"He's not who I expected him to be."	Disappointed
"What am I supposed to do about this?"	Frustrated
"It's not that hard!"	Irritated

Now let's see how she might alter those thoughts and how her feelings would change accordingly:

Instead of...	Try this thought....	Olivia's feelings based on new thought
"Jordan will flunk out of school."	"Jordan's really struggling in middle school."	Concerned
"He's not who I expected him to be."	"Jordan is in metamorphosis: he's not yet who he will be."	Patient
"What am I supposed to do about this?"	"We'll need to work together on this."	Collaborative
"It's not that hard!"	"It's different from when I went to school."	Compassionate

We can see that if Olivia breaks down her initial general and inflammatory thoughts, she comes up with a specific set of thoughts, each of which evokes a more specific feeling than that of anger. Then, when she reframes those more specific thoughts into less negative ones, she begins to feel differently, and more compassionately, about her son. Let's do this exercise one more time, with Abbie:

Instead of . . .	Feeling	Try this thought	Abbie's new feeling
"It doesn't make sense not to turn your homework in."	Confused	"I wonder what prevented him from turning in the assignments."	Concerned
"Kevin is 'devolving.' "	Disappointed	"Kevin is in metamorphosis: he's not yet who he will be."	Patient

Instead of . . .	Feeling	Try this thought	Abbie's new feeling
"I can't believe he's missing *six* assignments!"	Incredulous	"He must be pretty overwhelmed to have not turned in so many assignments."	Compassionate
"If he can't even walk up to the teacher and hand in his assignments, what can I do?"	Helpless	"I wonder if I can help him feel more confident about approaching the teacher."	Helpful

The exercise of breaking into the "thoughts window" is not one that can be done in the heat of the moment. Rather, it's a proactive device to be used once you discover that you're in a negative cycle with your preteen. Many parents even find it helpful to "chart out" their think-feel-do cycle in a calmer moment so that they can effectively make a shift to more neutral feelings.

The Second "Window": Action. The second window where we can break into a negative cycle with our middle schooler lies in what action we take: what we *do* when a problem arises. For many, this window is easier to use, because it can be taken advantage of no matter what our thoughts or feelings are about a specific situation.

Changing a cycle by changing what we do in any given situation requires learning and using the techniques presented throughout this book. When we have a handle on a variety of tools, we can communicate with our preteen effectively in spite of our feelings.

Here's how that might look in Olivia's case, even if she doesn't analyze and change her thoughts about the situation:

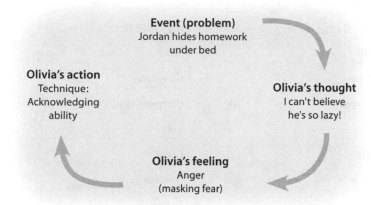

HELPING THE OVERWHELMED SLACKER

Children who feel overwhelmed often become discouraged and begin to lose the confidence necessary to take the risks involved in breaking out of their own cycles. Their lack of academic success becomes a self-fulfilling prophecy: they're overwhelmed; they do less work; they feel more overwhelmed and begin to believe that they're simply not capable of keeping up with the other students; this overwhelms them more; and so on.

One possible way to help them break out of their cycle is to point out their strengths. We call this "acknowledging ability."

The Skill of Acknowledging Ability

To use this skill, focus first on the activities at which your middle schooler succeeds or areas in which he seems to have specific strengths. Break down academics into smaller pieces; think about creative and interpersonal abilities as well. Here is a partial list to stimulate your thinking:

My child is good at:	My child is...
Math	Kind
English	Generous
Languages	Compassionate
Science	Polite
Sports	Creative
History	Helpful
Dance	Funny
Art	Loving
Writing	Cooperative
Computers	Responsible

Each of these skills or abilities could be broken down even further. For example, English can be broken into vocabulary, grammar, handwriting, and the like. Compassion can be broken down into compassion with peers, siblings, animals, elderly people, and so forth.

It's important to think in terms of the large variety of characteristics, skills, talents, and abilities that make your middle schooler who he is as a whole person. Otherwise, you'll begin to see him as a label, much as Olivia is doing when she says Jordan is "lazy." When we remove the labels from our preteens and honor their individual and specific strengths, we can then communicate those strengths to them. When we acknowledge ability, it helps to restore our middle schooler's confidence.

Olivia decided to try this with Jordan. She acknowledged that while he was struggling with completing homework assignments, he was actually doing well on his math tests. In addition, she recognized that he is a talented basketball player and loyal team member. To use the skill of "acknowledging ability" and to make it even more powerful, she wrote her thoughts in a "love ticket."

Combine the technique of "love tickets" with
"acknowledging ability" for more powerful results.

That night, she left a love ticket for Jordan on his pillow that said, "Dear Jordan, I appreciate your skill in math—I always know I can turn to you when I have a question, especially about fractions!"

The following day, she texted him, "FYI, I love you!"

On the third night (which happened to be after a basketball game), she wrote, "To my 'team player': you really know how to focus to meet your goals!"

Jordan approached her on the fourth day and asked, "Mom? What's with the notes?"

Olivia replied, "You know, Jordan, I just realized that I don't necessarily compliment you enough on all the things you do well, and I also wanted to say 'I love you' more often. So, when I find myself thinking about you during the day, I put it in writing so I won't forget to tell you."

"Oh," Jordan said, seeming nonplussed but accepting, and walked away.

Olivia kept writing the notes, not every day, but several times a week.

Carpe Diem

At the same time that Olivia was beginning to "acknowledge ability" for Jordan, Abbie was using the same skill with Kevin. Rather than writing him love tickets, however, she decided to simply acknowledge his strengths verbally. This involves adopting a mind-set of "catching him doing it right." In some ways, this is more difficult, because it means you have to think quickly enough to acknowledge a strength when you see it displayed.

Abbie began to look for opportunities to acknowledge ability with Kevin. She noticed that when he did his homework, he spread it out and organized it by subject into piles. She decided to seize the opportunity to compliment him: "Hey, Kev, I don't mean to interrupt, but I just wanted to say that it looks as if you have a great system going there." Kevin grunted, and Abbie left.

Later, she checked back in and noticed that a number of assignments had been completed. She patted him on the back and said, "Plowing through, I see!"

Respect your child's need to talk at his own pace.

After he finished his homework, he came into the living room where she was sitting. "I'm finished," he said. "Can I watch TV now?"

"Sure," said Abbie. "Looks as if your organization paid off. That was a lot of work, and you got through all of it!" Click. The TV went on. Abbie went back to her newspaper, and Kevin sat watching the screen.

At the next commercial, Kevin said, "Hey, Mom?"

"Yeah?" Abbie replied.

"I'm a little discouraged."

"About what?" Abbie asked.

"Well," said Kevin, "it's just that school is so rushed."

"Really?" asked Abbie. "Tell me more about that."

"Well, it's just that we have all these classes—and all this stuff that has to be turned in. And I can keep track of it at home. . . . Oh, wait, the show's back on." Kevin's eyes went back to the TV.

Abbie was tempted to ask him to turn it off to continue their conversation, but instinct told her that it was probably better to wait. When the next commercial came up, she said, "So, you were saying that there's a lot of stuff to keep track of?"

"Oh, yeah," Kevin said, picking up the thread. "And so, at the end of the class, I sometimes don't have time to get my homework out of my backpack and give it to the teacher. And she's busy, and there's, like, a whole bunch of kids around her, and so, then I just leave. It's like I can be organized at home, but not at school."

For Abbie and Kevin, "acknowledging ability" opened Kevin up to talking about the problem he was having. Because Abbie had been specific about his strengths, he was able to take the next step and contrast how organized he was at home with his lack of organization at school. Abbie also used the skill of "listening with heart," which we spoke about in Chapter 1, when Kevin was speaking. This allowed the door of communication to remain open.

The Skill of "Cooperative Communication"

Whether "acknowledging ability" opens your child up immediately (as with Kevin) or not (as with Jordan), it allows you to then use the next skill: "cooperative communication."

Cooperative communication draws directly on three of the four qualities of parenting.a middle schooler: respect, support, and collaboration. The three-step process looks like this:

- ◄ **Respect** your child's feelings as legitimate, and acknowledge them.
- ◄ **Support** your child by helping him brainstorm solutions.
- ◄ **Collaborate** with your child by offering to help him create a plan that meets the needs of both of you.

Let's see how Abbie continues her conversation with Kevin and uses cooperative communication:

"It sounds as if the rush to get from class to class can be pretty overwhelming."

"Yeah," Kevin says, his eyes drifting back to the television.

Abbie laughs and says, "It also looks as if there might be a better time to talk about this. Do you want to talk after this show is over?"

Kevin looks relieved. "OK, yeah. Thanks, Mom."

Abbie's respect for Kevin is evident here, not only in her acknowledgment of his feelings but also in her allowing him to finish watching his show.

When the show is over and the TV is turned off, Mom starts the conversation again. "So, anyway, middle school can feel kind of overwhelming, huh?"

"Totally!" Kevin says.

"Well," Abbie empathizes, "I get that. I mean, you have—what?— seven classes a day?" Kevin nods. "And it's not just about doing the work, which you clearly are organized about, but it's also about figuring out how to get that work back to the teacher when things are so rushed and chaotic."

"That's it!" Kevin exclaims.

"Hmmm . . . " says Abbie. "Well, I wonder if we could come up with a plan together so that you can feel more organized at school?"

> **Brainstorming:**
> Begin with, "I wonder if . . . " or "What do
> you think would happen if . . . "

Kevin nods. "OK, but what?"

"What do you think would happen if you had a file in your backpack that was just for homework and it was divided by subject? I noticed that you do that here at home when you're doing the homework."

"But how's that going to help?" Kevin asks.

"Well, maybe it won't," Abbie acknowledges, "but it seems to me that you could then carry it around from class to class, and you could leave your backpack in your locker. Then, at the end of class, you wouldn't have to search your whole backpack; you could just look in the right section and pull out what you need without having to think too much about it."

Kevin looks thoughtful. "It might work . . . "

Abbie shrugs. "And if it doesn't, we'll come up with something else, I'm sure."

"OK, can we go buy the file now?" Kevin asks.

Kevin tried the solution and found it worked. Over time, he made some modifications, but it got him back on track turning in his homework and getting credit for the work he was actually doing.

The Gift of Acceptance

With Olivia and Jordan, the road was longer. Because Kevin already had a level of organization at home, he was ahead of the game. Olivia would need to begin her "cooperative communication" with appropriate expectations. Jordan might never be as organized as Kevin, and his strength might never be academic. If she expects Jordan to be a great scholar, he may always fall short of that expectation and give up trying at all. And if he stops trying, he really will fail.

> **Manage your expectations:**
> Don't expect your middle schooler to "hit
> a home run" if the child can barely make
> contact with the ball.

When we are able to recognize our children's strengths and weaknesses, we can appreciate and accept our children for who they are. It's then that they reach their potential. I'm reminded of one parent who entertained thoughts of her daughter's becoming a prima ballerina. Then, her daughter suffered an accident that temporarily confined her to a wheelchair and guaranteed years of physical therapy. The mother said to me, "All I'm hoping for now is normal: a regular job, good friends, a home. Nothing special. Just normal: that's all I pray for."

Accepting that your child may "just be normal" is one of the greatest gifts that you can give to him.

Olivia Uses "Cooperative Communication"

Over time, Olivia came to a point where she accepted that there would be many career paths and much happiness available to Jordan, even if he didn't get straight As (or even Bs) in school. Still, it was obvious that he was clearly feeling bad about himself because of his lack of organization and failing grades, so Olivia decided to try the "cooperative communication" skill. I've bracketed the different steps to make it clear how she's using the technique.

Late one evening, Jordan is getting ready for bed, and Olivia comes into his room. "Hey, buddy, can I have a word?" she asks. Jordan puts aside the sports magazine he's reading and says, "Yeah, sure."

[**Respect what your child is going through.**] "I've been talking to some of the other moms, and they say that middle school is pretty overwhelming."

"Boy, is *that* true," Jordan sighs.

"Yeah, I guess I didn't realize that it had changed so much since I was in middle school."

"It has?" Jordan looks surprised.

[**Acknowledge feelings.**] "It sure has!" Olivia responds. "When I was in middle school, we had maybe four textbooks. There weren't any Xeroxes, so we almost never got handouts to take home. You guys have more classes, *and* you have to keep track of all those papers in addition to your textbooks. It must be completely overwhelming for you!"

"It is, Mom. It's completely overwhelming. I don't even know how to begin to keep track of stuff."

[**Begin brainstorming.**] "I can sure understand that!" Olivia replies. "If I were your age, I wouldn't have a clue. *I wonder if* we could work together to see if we could come up with a strategy for you?"

Jordan suddenly looks sullen and responds, "Aw, Mom. Nothing will help. I'm just not a good student."

**Acknowledge ability
and make a connection with the thing
that your child is struggling with.**

"You're a good basketball player," Olivia responds.

Looking confused, Jordan asks, "What does that have to do with anything?"

[**Continue brainstorming.**] "Well, that takes organization, and you have to think on your feet. I wonder if there's a way to apply the skills you already have on the court to what you would like to achieve in school?"

Jordan looks suspicious. "They're totally different," he tells her.

[**Collaborate by offering to help create a plan.**] "Maybe," Olivia says with a shrug. "In any case, do you want to try? Not now, I mean, but maybe tomorrow. You could explain basketball a little bit more to me, and we could see if it would help. If it doesn't, it doesn't; no harm done. At least I'll learn a little more about the game!"

"You'll *never* understand it!" Jordan teases and adds, "You're terrible with sports."

Olivia laughs. "Yeah," she says, "well, that's why I need you to help! I'll see you in the morning."

Olivia does a lovely job here. She paces her communication so that it doesn't overwhelm Jordan, and, most important, she doesn't try to accomplish the creation of a plan in one sitting. In the end, she even skillfully turns it around by implying that she's the one who needs help, rather than Jordan.

In the ensuing days, Olivia followed up with Jordan, who began to explain the principles of basketball to her. In addition to many other tidbits, she learned that the coach consulted with the players before the game to create a game plan, which involved deciding what tactics would be employed during the game. Olivia connected this concept with academics, suggesting that maybe she and Jordan could come up with a game plan for homework. Eventually, they decided together that Jordan could sort his homework into three piles: dribble, pass, and shoot. "Dribble" homework would be the homework he needed to work on a little bit at a time throughout the week. "Pass" homework would be the homework he needed to get more information on before completing it—from either the teacher, classmates, the Internet, or a book. "Shoot" homework was homework he needed to do that evening to turn in the next day.

Even if an idea sounds "corny" to an adult,
when a middle schooler thinks of it himself
(or in a brainstorming session with Mom
or Dad), he's likely to follow through.

Things went more smoothly after that. Jordan and Olivia had a "team meeting" every Monday after school, with a follow-up on Wednesday. Jordan's grades improved once he was turning in all of his homework. He never did become a straight-A student, but he did well enough to get into college and is planning a career as a high school basketball coach.

3

How to Break the Nagging Cycle and Turn Responsibility Over to Your Middle Schooler

Samantha, a bright, energetic mom in her early forties, looks dejected when she arrives at our parenting group. Her normal, upbeat energy is missing this morning, and she collapses into a chair. "I've had it," she says bleakly. "Honestly, I'm completely overwhelmed with Nick. I haven't felt this way since he was a toddler." The group looks at her expectantly. She shakes her head in disbelief. "I can't get him to brush his teeth in the morning. I know that sounds small, and stupid and crazy, but it's driving me nuts."

The group nods empathetically. They understand Samantha's exhaustion, because, while arguing with your child about brushing his teeth in the morning may be a "small" thing, it's not insignificant or uncommon.

Another mom, normally easygoing and calm, speaks up, her voice agitated: "Why do they do this? I don't understand it. I'm having a similar problem with Asanti. I ask her if she's done something—it could be anything: brushing her teeth, putting her homework in her bag, anything—and she scowls and gets this attitude and says, 'I can't believe you don't *trust* me,' and then she storms off. Of course, then I feel guilty for not trusting her, but you know what? She doesn't deserve my trust, because a lot of the time, she says she did something, but she really didn't! With that track record, why should I trust her?"

Why indeed? And why is it that elementary school children can go from willingly accepting instructions from Mom or Dad to brush their teeth, put on a jacket, shower, and all the other myriad things we ask them to do on a daily basis to being middle schoolers who resist (sometimes vehemently) these gentle reminders?

FEELINGS RUN DEEP

The answer is that middle schoolers feel things more deeply than ever before, and they often take our comments very personally. In a developmental period during which their very sense of who they are is rapidly changing, simple queries are heard as nagging. Gentle reminders are heard as insults. Thus, when Mom or Dad asks a simple question about teeth brushing or putting books in a bag, what the preteen hears is markedly different from what the parent actually says.

Let's take a look at some of the interpretations that preteens might make from a simple question by Mom or Dad:

What you say	What they hear
"Did you brush your teeth?"	"You can't look after yourself."
"Is your homework in your bag?"	"I don't trust you."
"Did you shower?"	"You look/smell bad."
"Have you finished your homework?"	"You're a poor student."

Clearly, when Asanti retaliated with "I can't believe you don't trust me," she was responding to what she thought she heard, not to what Mom actually said. And Nick, rather than talking back to his mother, chose to resist brushing his teeth in an effort to prove that he's independent.

"Well, what am I supposed to do?" Samantha asks. "Am I supposed to just let him go without brushing his teeth? Let him get the cavities? Will he learn then?"

NATURAL CONSEQUENCES

Samantha's question is a good one. Natural consequences—those things that happen as a direct result of our children's actions without parental interference—can be powerful teachers. Think about it: how many times does a toddler touch a hot stove? Only once, if at all. Why? The direct result of the action is uncomfortable, and the child learns quickly from discomfort.

Sometimes it's appropriate to allow our middle schoolers to learn from the natural consequences of their actions. For example, if Asanti's mother, Adanna, resisted asking her daughter whether she'd put her homework in her bag, Asanti would go to school without the homework. The result—either a reprimand from the teacher or a lower grade—would be uncomfortable, and she'd likely learn from the natural consequences to take more care the next time. Sometimes, of course, natural consequences won't work. Hearken back to both Jordan and Kevin from Chapter 2, for whom the natural consequences weren't enough to break their cycles of disorganization. However, trying natural consequences can be an important first step, especially because they're such powerful teachers. Many parents are wary about allowing their children to experience the natural consequences of their actions—worrying that their child will "fail." And of course, we don't want that to happen.

But we're not talking about drowning here, and it's OK to let them sink a few times. Going to school without her homework once, or even twice, is unlikely to cause Asanti to flunk a class. As parents, though, we find it easy to project the worst-case scenario onto our children. We love them so much, and that love is often accompanied by fear that they won't reach their potential. So, the one time they neglect to turn in a piece of homework, we translate that to flunking out of school. The one time they lose their coat, we think it means they'll "never" be responsible.

> **The Natural Consequences Technique:** It's OK to let your child sink sometimes.

The mistakes that our preteens make are an inevitable and integral part of the learning process. In *The Blessing of a Skinned Knee: Using Jewish Teachings to Raise Self-Reliant Children*, Wendy Mogel observes that parents behave as if we're cruise directors on a ship and our job is to make sure our children grow up with as few bumps as possible. She goes on to say that this is the worst possible mistake we can make. She asserts, "Our job is to raise our children to leave us. The children's job is to find their own path in life. If they stay carefully protected in the nest of the family, children will become weak and fearful or feel too comfortable to want to leave."

THE SANDWICH TECHNIQUE

Whenever possible, then, it's best to allow our preteen to experience the natural consequences of his or her choices. There are, of course, exceptions: when the consequences may be dangerous, or unhealthy, as in the case of Nick's not brushing his teeth, or when the natural consequences don't have an effect, as in the cases of Jordan and Kevin, then we as parents have a duty to step in.

How we do this involves first setting ourselves up for success. We've already seen that virtually the last thing to which middle schoolers will respond positively is the direct approach. In order to have them "hear" the importance of teeth brushing, we must present the problem to our children in a positive way. Mary Pipher, in her book *The Shelter of Each Other: Rebuilding Our Families*, recommends the "Sandwich Technique."

The "sandwich technique" is a communication skill that allows us to frame our values, concerns, even criticisms, in a way that our preteen can hear them without feeling defensive. The first step (the "bread" on the bottom of the sandwich) lies in formulating a positive statement to our child. For example, Samantha might say the following to Nick: "You know, Nick, I really appreciate how independent you're becoming. You've started taking a lot of responsibility in a number of areas."

The Sandwich Technique: The first piece of bread is a positive, honest statement.

This first statement needn't be long, but it must be honest. Preteens have finely tuned radar for dishonesty or manipulation. If our middle schooler believes we're saying something only in order to manipulate him into behaving in a certain way, he will tune us out. If Samantha feels that she can't, in all honesty, say that Nick is becoming independent in other areas, she should formulate her first statement differently—perhaps by saying: "I know how much you hate my nagging, Nick, and I'm really trying to cut down. You're a trustworthy kid, and it's just going to take me a while to catch up to the 'new' and more grown-up Nick."

Some parents are surprised to discover that learning to formulate positive, honest statements can take practice. The good news is twofold, though: first, our children give us plenty of opportunities for practice; and second, much of their behavior is repetitive.

Script Yourself

Repetitive behavior gives us an advantage in that we can "script" ourselves in advance. Scripting involves being a "proactive" rather than a "reactive" parent. The difference between the two is that reactive parents wait for an issue to come up and then try to handle it on the spot. Proactive parents, on the other hand, think ahead and plan carefully so that their interventions and communications with their children are effective.

In Samantha and Nick's case, then, Samantha knows that the teeth-brushing problem is likely to occur every morning. This gives her the opportunity to create and memorize a script, based on the sandwich technique, and to sit down with Nick in the afternoon or evening to talk to him, when feelings are less likely to be running high.

> **The Script Technique:** Be proactive and use
> a "script" to get your point across.

"I Statements"

The next part of the script is the "meat" of the sandwich. Here is where we can express our concerns to our middle schooler. In the "meat" of the sandwich, it's important for us to take ownership of our concerns by using what's called an "I statement." These "I statements" reflect personal responsibility rather than pointing the finger of blame. They contrast sharply with "You statements," which will make the preteen feel defensive and angry.

Here are examples of both:

"I statement"	"You statement"
"I feel a little concerned about teeth brushing."	"You don't seem to be brushing your teeth in the morning."
"I'm confused about whether your homework is getting turned in on time."	"You aren't taking responsibility for your homework."
"I feel bewildered about what you just said."	"You're lying to me."

As you can see, "I statements" start with the word *I*, and "You statements" start with the word *you*. However, don't make the mistake of believing that just beginning a statement with the word *I* automatically makes it an "I statement." For example, "I think you're lying about brushing your teeth in the morning" is a "You statement" disguised as an "I statement." What differentiates the true "I statement" from the disguised "I statement" is that true "I statements" don't point the finger of blame; they take responsibility for our feelings about a situation. Thus, "I statements" must include a feeling word as well as beginning with a self-reference.

> **The Sandwich Technique:** The meat of the sandwich is "I statements."

Feeling Words

We create powerful "I statements" when we use the wealth of feeling words available to us, rather than sticking to what I call "umbrella feelings," the five or six common feeling words with which we are the most comfortable and that we use the most often. While you may have your own umbrella "set," here are the ones most people use: angry, sad, scared, overwhelmed, frustrated, upset, and happy.

The problem with using only umbrella feelings is that our children can become desensitized to them. After numerous "I statements" in which a parent says, "I feel upset that . . . " the preteen is bound to think (or say), "Well, you're *always* upset, so what does it matter?"

It's far more effective to branch out, to use all of the various words that are available to us. Here is a list of possibilities:

Pleasant feelings		Unpleasant feelings	
accepted	adequate	afraid	angry
adventurous	amused	anxious	apathetic
bold	brilliant	ashamed	bashful

Pleasant feelings		Unpleasant feelings	
calm	caring	bored	cautious
cheered	comfortable	cheated	concerned
confident	content	confused	cranky
creative	daring	defeated	defiant
delighted	eager	disappointed	discouraged
elated	encouraged	domineering	down
energetic	enthusiastic	embarrassed	envious
excited	fascinated	foolish	frustrated
free	full	guilty	hateful
glad	great	hesitant	hopeless
gutsy	happy	hurt	impatient
helpful	high	irritated	jealous
hopeful	humble	let-down	lonely
important	inspired	miserable	nervous
joyful	lovely	overwhelmed	overworked
loving	overjoyed	pained	possessive
peaceful	peppy	pressured	provoked
playful	pleased	pushed	rejected
proud	refreshed	remorseful	resentful
relieved	satisfied	shy	skeptical
secure	snappy	stupid	suspicious
sophisticated	successful	threatened	tired
surprised	sympathetic	trapped	uncomfortable
tender	tranquil	uneasy	unhappy
understood	warm	unloved	unsure
wonderful	zany	weary	worried

Here are a few possibilities for Samantha's "I statement" to Nick:

◄ "One area that I feel concerned about is teeth brushing."
◄ "I'm unsure about whether you're brushing your teeth every morning."

◄ "I'm a little worried that you might be skipping your teeth brushing in the morning and developing cavities."

Avoid Using the Word *But*

As we cover the first piece of "bread" with the "meat of the sandwich," it's important that we not connect the two with the word *but*.

Connecting "bread" to "meat" the right way	Connecting "bread" to "meat" the wrong way
"You know, Nick, I really appreciate how independent you're becoming. I'm a little worried that you might be skipping your teeth brushing in the morning and developing cavities."	"You know, Nick, I really appreciate how independent you're becoming, **but** I'm a little worried that you might be skipping your teeth brushing in the morning and developing cavities."

The word *but* negates everything that comes before it. Thus, the child would hear the concern or criticism, but not the positive statement about his independence. This would put him on the defensive and be less effective.

Putting It All Together

Once we formulate our "I statement," it's time to put the second piece of bread on the "sandwich." As with the first piece of bread, the second should be a positive statement, preferably one that projects trust about how things will go in the future.

The Sandwich Technique:
The second piece of bread is a positive statement or statement of trust.

Samantha might say: "I'm sure we can work out a way that I can support your independence around this issue and stop nagging. What do you think?"

Notice how Samantha finishes with a question. This helps engage the preteen in the communication process and makes it more likely for him to take ownership of a solution, should one be reached. However, the question is not absolutely necessary to the "sandwich." Samantha could just as easily say, "I trust that you'll be self-reliant in this area, since you're already accepting responsibility in so many other ways."

EXHIBITING TRUST

Trust is a crucial part of the relationship between parent and middle schooler. If we act as though our preteen isn't trustworthy, then there's no reason for him to act responsibly. His thought will be, "Well, Mom/Dad doesn't trust me anyway, so why should I make an effort to be trusted?"

Exhibiting trust is often a matter of perspective. It's somewhat like seeing a glass as half full instead of half empty. When we're in doubt about whether our preteen is fulfilling a responsibility, or when she is "doing it right" at least some of the time, we want to use the skill of exhibiting trust to communicate our positive expectations.

> **Exhibiting Trust: Calling the glass half full instead of half empty.**

This brings us back to Adanna's question about Asanti, who asks to be trusted but then breaks trust by not doing what she says she has done. Adanna's first step with Asanti should be to use the sandwich technique. She might say:

[**Bread**] "Asanti, I really appreciate your growing desire for independence, and when I nag, it probably seems as if I don't trust you. Trust is important in our relationship, and I'm going to work on not nagging so I can show you how much I do trust you. [**Meat**] I can't help feeling a little concerned that your homework might not be getting into your schoolbag each morning, and that showing up without it will lead to lower grades than you deserve. [**Bread**] You're a good student, and I know that you'll take this responsibility seriously."

After Adanna has used the sandwich technique, she should quietly observe to see how Asanti is doing. At this point, it's critical that Adanna *stop nagging*. She needs to give Asanti a chance to either sink or prove herself. Any breach in exhibiting trust will serve as proof to Asanti that Adanna didn't really mean what she said and that she doesn't really trust her after all.

If Asanti does indeed "sink" once or twice, if she comes home bemoaning the teacher's "unfairness" in giving her a lower grade because she turned in a piece of homework after its deadline, it's imperative that Adanna refrain from saying, "I told you so." "I told you so" ruins natural consequences.

Instead of saying, "I told you so," Asanti could use "exhibiting trust": "How disappointing for you. I'm so sorry it worked out that way. You're a good student, though, Asanti, and I know that you'll figure out a way to get the grade you think you deserve."

> "I told you so" ruins natural consequences. Use the "exhibiting trust" technique instead.

THE TRUST CONTRACT

What if after Asanti has sunk once or twice, however, it becomes apparent to Adanna that her daughter is beginning to drown? Then it's time to set up a "trust contract." With middle schoolers, it is essential to initially give trust freely, but once trust is broken, it then must be earned back.

Our children desperately want us to trust them. Loss of our trust represents a powerful consequence for inappropriate behavior. This is true, however, only if they've experienced the benefits of our trust in the past, which is why it's so important that we give them our trust freely to begin with. If and only if they breach that trust should they then have to prove that they're trustworthy.

The first step in setting up a "trust contract" is to think through the following questions:

- ◄ How much time is needed for our middle schooler to earn back our trust?
- ◄ What action can we take to ensure that trust isn't being broken?

The amount of time required for a middle schooler to earn back trust, as well as what action we take, will often depend on the severity of the infraction. For example, one mother's son stole some items from cars in a parking lot. This is a serious infraction. She set up a period of two months for him to earn her trust back. Having a specific time line such as this is important. If the probationary period is ambiguous, the middle schooler will feel defeated, as if he's climbing a mountain with no end. If he feels defeated and becomes discouraged, he will likely give up and revert back to untrustworthy actions.

> **Set a reasonable time frame. Create a logical way for your preteen to earn back your trust.**

The action that we decide on should be logically related to however the child has broken trust. As for the mother whose son vandalized cars, she curtailed his independence by walking him to and from school every day and accompanying him on any extracurricular activities that he had planned. Her rationale for this was that he hadn't behaved responsibly when she allowed him freedom and independence, so the result was that his freedom and independence would be decreased until she felt he was trustworthy once more. By creating this kind of logical relationship, we help our middle schoolers learn to evaluate the consequences and modify their behavior accordingly. For this mother and son, there were also times when the child's activities conflicted with her plans. Rather than follow him around like a puppy dog and inconvenience herself, she made him cancel his activities.

If Samantha needs to set up a trust contract for Nick's not brushing his teeth, any of the following actions would be logical:

◄ Check his toothbrush every morning to see if it's wet.
◄ Check his teeth every morning to make sure they look clean.
◄ Schedule a dental appointment at the end of the week to have the dentist determine whether proper hygiene is being maintained.

If Adanna needs to set up a trust contract for Asanti's not putting her homework in her bag, she might decide to use one of the following logically related actions:

◄ Check Asanti's bag each morning to make sure the homework is there.
◄ Ask Asanti's teacher to send her an e-mail every day to report about whether the homework is present.
◄ Supervise every evening so that she sees Asanti putting the homework in her bag.

Clearly, the issues that Samantha and Adanna are having with their middle schoolers are not anywhere near as serious as breaking into cars and stealing. Therefore, each might set up a period of one week or less for her preteen to earn back trust.

Presenting the Trust Contract

Equally important to the content of the contract is the method of presentation. Trust contracts are not meant to punish or control our children, but rather to engage our children in a relationship with us so that we can support them in growing up. Trust should always be viewed and communicated as a valued commodity in the household. The more responsible you are, the more trust you engender.

**The "trust contract": Combine
techniques you've already learned.**

When we present the trust contract to our children, it's important to come from a relationship perspective. This means utilizing some of the techniques you've learned thus far: "I statements," "sandwiching," and "scripting."

For example, Adanna might script herself during the day and approach Asanti on the weekend:

["**I statement**"] "Asanti, I feel extremely concerned about the fact that I've trusted you to put your homework in your bag and you've now forgotten three times. [**Bread of sandwich**] I believe that this is something you can remember to do without my nagging. [**Meat of sandwich**] I'm going to ask you to earn my trust back in this regard, [**Bread of sandwich**] which I'm sure that you can do, because you're a trustworthy kid. [**Length of time**] For the next three days, [**Action**] I'm going to check your bag every morning to make sure your work is there. [**Garnish!**] At the end of that time, I know you'll prove to me that you're trustworthy, and my trust in you will be restored. At that point I'll stop checking.

Sometimes parents worry that using the script technique makes them sound phony. This is understandable. Remember that as a parent of a preteen, you're essentially learning a new language to deal with the "foreigner" in your house. If you were learning Russian, Chinese, or any other language that's new to you, you would sound stilted and insecure at first. You would need to practice the phrases you were learning over and over again to "get it right" and make it sound smooth and natural. It would take time for you to become fluent. The same is true of your communication techniques with your middle schooler.

> Remember that learning a
> new "language" takes time. It may sound
> "phony" to you at first.

If you're worried that your child will think you're odd for speaking in this new way, there's no problem with presenting it to him by saying something like, "I'm learning a new way to speak to you respectfully that will honor your growing independence. It's new to me, though, and it might sound funny for a while. I hope you'll be patient as I learn."

Wrapping It Up by "Acknowledging Effort"

Finally, it's important to acknowledge when our children are making progress. This act of "acknowledging effort" should be performed both during and at the end of the trust contract.

> Use "acknowledging effort"
> throughout your parenting to encourage your
> preteen's step-by-step progress.

Thus, Samantha and Adanna should make sure to acknowledge progress during the length of time that the contract is in place. Samantha might say, "You're doing a great job restoring my trust. Only two more days to go."

When trust is restored in full, this should be acknowledged as well: "I knew you could do it. You've regained my full trust. Great work."

HOW'D THEY DO?

Let's hear how the parents and preteens in this chapter finally worked things out.

Samantha and Nick

Samantha approached Nick without feeling the need to script herself. She chose to time her intervention when Nick's basketball team had just won an important game and Nick was feeling especially proud of his contribution.

She used the sandwich technique and said, "You know, this is just one more example of how competent you're becoming, Nick. You must feel so proud of yourself, just as I feel proud of you too. And I know this seems completely out of the blue, but I've noticed that I've been nagging you about certain things, and I realize that I just don't need to do that so much anymore. It'll take me a while to get used to it, but I'm going to make a start and stop nagging you about brushing your teeth in the mornings. I know that you don't need me to do that and that you'll be as competent in that as you are in so many other ways."

Nick looked surprised and said, "Well, thanks, Mom."

Samantha spent the next week observing, and she reported that while Nick didn't brush his teeth every morning, he managed five out of seven days, which was much better than before. She then used "acknowledging effort" by saying, "I have to tell you I noticed that you remembered to brush your teeth without my nagging this week."

While it may have been tempting for Samantha to mention that Nick missed two days, she resisted being perfectionistic and was satisfied with the fact that Nick had made progress. Sure enough, her trust that the progress would continue paid off, and in the second week and beyond, Nick became entirely responsible and brushed his teeth every morning.

Avoid perfectionism.

Adanna and Asanti

Adanna had a tougher time with Asanti. Because Asanti's general nature is more defiant than Nick's, Adanna felt she needed to "cut to the chase" and begin with a trust contract. She spent several days working out a script that felt comfortable and decided that when she sat down with Asanti, she would have some "cues" written down to help her remember how she wanted to phrase the contract.

She said, "Asanti, I realize that you're getting older and that I may still be treating you like a much younger child. I don't want to do that anymore, and my guess is that you don't want me to do that either."

Asanti nodded but looked suspicious as her mother continued.

"I know I've been nagging you about putting your homework in your bag every night. I'd like to trust that you can do that yourself. What I want to do is set up a sort-of 'trust contract' with you . . . "

Asanti broke in: "You *don't* trust me. I've been trying to tell you that. You *never* believe *anything* I say I'm going to do."

Adanna took a deep breath and, utilizing the "listening with heart" skill from Chapter 1, said, "Tell me what you mean."

Asanti's eyes narrowed, and her tone became sarcastic. "Tell me what you mean," she said, her voice mimicking her mother. "I'll *tell* you what I mean. I *tell* you over and over again that I'm going to put my homework in my bag. And then you ask me *again*. And I tell you I'm not done, but do you hear that? Nooooo. You're always so focused on making sure everything is under control that you *never* hear a word I say and you *never* trust me."

It would have been easy for Adanna to take Asanti's "bait"—the sarcastic tone she used when she mimicked her mother's words. To Adanna's credit, however, she didn't bite; instead, she continued to "listen with heart." She'd already discovered that "hugging a porcupine" isn't easy but that sometimes it's the best way to achieve our goals.

Hugging a porcupine isn't easy.
Avoid "rising to the bait."

"Wow, Asanti," Adanna said with concern, "I guess I didn't real-ize that I was being so controlling. I'd like to stop doing that."

"Yeah?" Asanti sneered. "How?"

"Well, I'm not exactly sure, because I've never done this before. What about if we make a deal? I'll promise that I won't ask you for an entire week about your homework, and we'll see how it goes, and you'll promise to 'meet' with me at the end of the week to give me feedback from your perspective."

"What happens if I say no?" Asanti asked.

"Well, nothing. I guess we just go back to the old way of doing things, with me nagging and both of us being unhappy."

Asanti thought for a moment and then said grudgingly, "Well, OK, I'll try it. But if you nag me, then I'm not meeting."

"That sounds fair," Adanna replied.

Notice that while the process was interrupted because of Asanti's defiance and anger, Adanna still got her "trust contract" communi-cated, albeit in a slightly different form from the one she originally intended. In addition, she didn't allow herself to be distracted from her goal by Asanti's challenging attitude, which was probably deliberate on Asanti's part. No doubt Asanti hoped that by distracting or anger-ing her mother, she could avoid having the conversation altogether.

At the end of the week, Asanti had managed to get her home-work in her bag twice but suffered "natural consequences" at school on two of the other mornings. Because Adanna kept her end of the trust bargain and didn't say anything, Asanti felt free to express her disappointment about her consequences when they met at the end of the week.

"I can't believe that I forgot to put my homework in my bag. The teacher lowered my grade *and* gave me extra work to do to make up for it. I guess I did better when you nagged me."

Adanna refused to buy into Asanti's negative attitude. Instead, she replied by "acknowledging effort": "No, you did remember some of the time. I'm sorry that you have extra work to do, but I'm sure it won't happen again. I know that you can do it."

"Thanks, Mom," Asanti replied. "I hope so."

By not allowing Asanti to slip into a negative state of mind ("I did better when you nagged me"), Adanna was able to break out of the nagging cycle of distrust in which they'd been engaged. The following week, she again kept her mouth shut, and Asanti remembered her homework every day.

The Boy Who Broke into Cars

Believe it or not, there was no fight about earning back parental trust in this case. Mom presented the trust contract matter-of-factly and unemotionally, and her son allowed her to accompany him to school and to his extracurricular activities for the two-month period. At the end of that time, Mom communicated that trust had been restored. Four years have now passed, and the boy has not done anything like that again. In fact, he is a responsible teen who works as a camp counselor with younger children each summer and is a trusted and valued member of the camp community.

4

Peer Pressure and Changing Values

"Mom, guess what?" thirteen-year-old Caley yells as she races across the threshold. "Leah got this really, really cool belly-button piercing, and so this weekend she's gonna show us where she got it, and it's really, really safe, and so we're gonna go, 'kay? Can I borrow from my allowance?"

Caley's mother, Dahlia, has three children: Caley, Hannah, and Liora. As she recounts this story about her oldest to our group, she looks furious. "Caley must be out of her mind!" she explodes. "She wants a piercing? A *belly-button* piercing?"

Scenarios like this make the hearts of parents freeze. Yet, during middle school, children begin to gravitate toward their peers and formulate a set of values that will help them differentiate themselves from their parents. This process completes itself within the four years of high school—resulting, it is hoped, in an independent young person ready to make her own way in the world. The process is normal, but the values-based choices that our middle schoolers are making are very different from the choices that we faced when we were their age.

Instead of choices about staying out past curfew in a relatively safe neighborhood, chatting on the phone longer than Mom or Dad would like, or talking back to their parents, middle schoolers have access to and are making choices about things such as multiple piercings, sexuality, smoking, and alcohol.

AREN'T THESE CHOICES CONFINED TO HIGH SCHOOL?

Times have changed. Extensive exposure to the media has introduced middle schoolers to values of which they previously might have been unaware until they reached high school.

According to the Kaiser Family Foundation, children spend more time (44.5 hours per week, or 6.5 hours daily) in front of computer, television, and game screens than any other activity in their lives except sleeping. It's no surprise, then, that the values communicated by the media are the ones that take precedence over family or school values. Moreover, in *U.S. News & World Report,* James McNeal says that with children under the age of twelve influencing the household spending of more than $600 billion annually, marketers are not shy about convincing middle schoolers of their prerogative to exert their influence. Preadolescents generalize that message and begin to believe that they have the maturity to make more grown-up choices—not just about money, but about their bodies, behavior, and relationships as well.

The need to "belong" to a peer group intensifies the pressure already exerted by the media. The kids are "grinding" at school dances, Mary gets a belly-button piercing, Don starts smoking . . . and our middle schooler begins to look like the odd one out if she doesn't participate in some way.

Of course, this can feel alarming to us as parents. And often the tendency is to put our foot down and say, "Absolutely not! As long as you live under my roof, you'll do as I say!" Unfortunately, this type of rigid attitude will likely backfire. Many of our children at this age have enough disposable income and enough freedom to sneak off and do what they want to do, with or without our consent. All they need is concrete evidence that we are adamantly opposed to something, and they have the ammunition to fulfill their developmental goal of proving they're different from us. So, if Dahlia were to react as strongly with Caley as she did within our parenting group and harshly criticize belly-button piercing, Caley might think, "Well, if she hates it so much, I'll be really different from her if I get it done anyway."

During these years, our job is to support the developmental process while still articulating our values and expectations in a way that's nonjudgmental yet influential.

THE SKILL OF "TELL ME MORE"

The key to remaining influential lies in adopting an attitude of curiosity about your preteen's ideas, philosophies, and values. If you approach her outrageous statements with a mind-set of "tell me more," you'll be surprised at how effectively you can influence her.

Before Dahlia realized that expressing her horror to Caley might have an adverse affect, she had indeed "lost it" and indicated that she thought the idea of a belly-button piercing was ridiculous. Now she wisely backtracks and makes an attempt to approach Caley with a "tell me more" philosophy.

She begins: "Caley, I'm sorry I reacted so strongly when you first told me about Leah's belly-button piercing. I was just caught off guard because I didn't realize that kids your age were getting that done. I'd like to start over, though. Would that be OK?"

Dahlia is smart to go back to Caley and not just drop the subject. Sometimes we'd like to pretend our middle schooler never brought something up, because we think it will just evaporate on its own. However, the likelihood is high that if we ignore the issue, it will actually simmer and eventually boil over into some sort of action.

You can always backtrack.

Caley's eyes narrow, but she says nothing.

Dahlia continues: "Why don't you tell me more about Leah's belly-button piercing. What does it look like?"

"You don't really want to know," Caley mutters. "You don't like anything my friends do."

"Oh, Caley, I'm sorry if I've given you that impression," Dahlia demurs. "I've never been the parent of a middle schooler before, and things were really different when I was your age, so I'm playing a lot of 'catch-up' here. I hope you can be patient with me while I figure this out."

Because Dahlia didn't initially keep her cool with Caley, she's having to do a bit of damage control to win back Caley's trust. The effort will be rewarded, however, if she can reinitiate the conversation without igniting rebellion.

"Well, OK," Caley says, swayed in part by her mother's humble tone. "It's just that it's really, really cool. It's a little turtle, and it has tiny crystal eyes. It's so cute, Mom, and I really want to get one."

Now that Caley is reengaged, Dahlia needs to proceed with caution and adhere strictly to the notion of "tell me more."

"A turtle does sound cute! Why don't you tell me more about it," Dahlia says. "Where did she get it done?"

"Ummm . . . I don't know, but she said it didn't hurt that much."

"Well, that's good. Did she say how much it cost?"

"No . . . "

"Hmmm . . . well, maybe we should go online just to find out a little more about it. What do you think?"

Notice that Dahlia is not giving Caley permission to pierce. She is, however, leading her on an investigation that goes beyond the "cool" factor into the more practical aspects of piercing.

Exploring Issues Together

Dahlia and Caley go online together to learn more about body piercing. As abhorrent as Dahlia finds it, she approaches the task much as a neutral reporter would if she were writing an article for a newspaper.

In the course of their investigation, both mother and daughter learn a lot about safety, how long the skin takes to heal, and the cost of piercing one's belly button. They also learn that minors must be accompanied by a parent. When they're finished, Dahlia asks Caley, "So, what do you think about what we've learned?"

Caley looks discouraged. "It's so much more expensive than I thought," she says, "and I didn't realize that it could take a whole year to heal. Maybe I'll wait after all."

This positive outcome (from Mom's perspective, at least) served as valuable reinforcement for Dahlia. Many parents fail to realize that if they exhibit some patience and nonjudgmentally help their preteen explore the value that she's espousing, it often leads to the middle schooler's rejecting, or at least postponing, the "new" or rebellious idea.

The Horror! The Horror!

Obviously, the hardest part of this skill is *not* reacting with horror when our middle schooler voices different values from ours. Keep in mind, though, that she hasn't behaved according to those values—so far; she's simply talking about them. This means that there's a small window of opportunity for us to exert our influence before she actually acts. Remaining nonjudgmental is the key.

Body language (which includes facial expression) is 55 percent of communication. Practice having a poker face so you don't give away that you're horrified.

"SANDWICHING" TO GET YOUR VALUES ACROSS

What if, however, Caley had not come around to Mom's point of view and had, instead, responded with, "See how cool it is, Mom? Will you come with me?"

In that case, Dahlia would need to use the "sandwich technique" from Chapter 3 to voice her values and concerns (I've underlined the "meat" of the sandwich): "I have to admit, Caley, that it can look quite beautiful. I'm really happy that we researched it together because it helped me get a little more perspective on it. I'm concerned about the amount of time it takes to heal, and the possibility of infection, particularly when you're at camp this summer. I'd like to wait to give my permission and think about it some more. How about if we talk about it again in the fall?"

In this "sandwich," Mom reinforces the appeal of the piercing ("it can look quite beautiful") before she states her concern. She also leaves the discussion open by setting a specific time line to reapproach the issue. This is important because it minimizes the possibility of Caley's rebelling.

Some parents worry that this approach is simply postponing the inevitable. You might think, "Wait a minute! Isn't Dahlia implying that she approves of Caley's getting her belly button pierced at a later time?"

The truth is that if Caley wants a piercing, she will ultimately get one, with or without Mom's approval. Remember that we're making an attempt to move from a "control approach" to a "relationship approach." Our job at this point is to reinforce our relationship with our middle schooler so that we might still influence her decision. By suggesting that we revisit the subject at a later time, we keep the lines of communication—and the possibility of influence—open.

Delaying the Decision

Many years ago, I had a parent who was adamantly opposed to letting her daughter get her ears pierced. Mentally, she'd decided that her daughter would need to be sixteen before she could make that decision. Rather than put her foot down unequivocally, however, she "sandwiched" and told her daughter that she wasn't comfortable and would like to revisit the subject in six months. When six months rolled around, she listened again to her daughter's request, using the skill of "tell me more." Again, she said she just wasn't comfortable, restating her concern about infection and the added responsibility of her daughter's keeping track of earrings. She said she'd continue to think about it and come back to it in another couple of months. This went on for years. By the time her daughter turned sixteen, she had changed her mind and decided that she preferred not to get her ears pierced after all.

Granted, there's no guarantee that things will work out exactly like this in your household, but it does go to show that a parent who listens with love and respect can exert a great deal of influence—far more than what comes from being rigid and controlling.

Putting Your Foot Down: A Word of Caution

Another mother in one of my groups was incredulous when I recommended "listening with heart" and using "tell me more" with our middle schoolers when they espouse values different from ours. She exclaimed vehemently, "I don't understand why we can't just put our foot down. I mean, when did we stop being the parent and start letting them run the show? I don't want to have a 'dialogue' about it.

Max has to know that as long as he's living in my house, he'll live by my rules."

Many parents feel flustered and resentful as this mother did, and it's hard to understand why we have to make the shift from controlling our middle schooler to engaging in a relationship with the child. To some, it feels as though these skills are the equivalent of coddling. Plus, it seems so much easier to "just say no." Perhaps we can learn something from the conclusion to this mother's story, though:

Throughout middle school and early high school, Gail continued to (in her words) "rule with an iron fist." Max had begun to pester her in eighth grade about getting one ear pierced, and Gail had steadfastly refused to practice either "listening with heart" or "tell me more." Instead, she continued to insist that as long as Max lived with her, he had to live by her rules. In Max's sophomore year of high school, he asked one more time for permission to pierce his ear. Gail said no again. Max left the house, and when he returned later that day, he had a full-arm tattoo.

We cannot win if we go up against our child's developmental drive to be different. Instead, we have to engage our respect for that process and work in relationship with our middle schooler to help him achieve his developmental goals in healthy ways.

RESPECTING YOUR PRETEEN'S CHANGING BIOLOGY

Ruth speaks up: "I am having trouble with Jeanne's going to bed way too late. Bedtime is supposed to be 9:30, and Jeanne is constantly arguing with me about it, saying that all her friends have later bedtimes and that I'm treating her like a baby."

Breaking with the normal routines is another way that preteens begin to push away from parental influence and test their growing independence. Wanting a later bedtime is further confounded by the fact that our middle schoolers' body clock may begin to change. According to the National Sleep Foundation, we are subject to "internal circadian biological clocks (which) regulate the timing of periods of sleepiness and wakefulness throughout the day." When a child enters adolescence, her circadian rhythm can shift, making it difficult for her to fall asleep prior to 11:00 P.M. Although Jeanne is only eleven, her body began to develop in fourth grade, and she got her period early in sixth grade. With preteens, it can be difficult to tell whether biology or peer pressure is at work when they argue to make certain changes.

For this reason, it's important for Ruth to respect the notion that Jeanne may actually be having difficulty falling asleep, not just wanting a later bedtime because "all her friends" have one. Still, Ruth needs to communicate with Jeanne about her concerns. One possible way to do this is by holding a family meeting.

WHAT ARE FAMILY MEETINGS?

Family meetings are a practical tool for encouraging family cohesion during middle school and beyond. Basically, they comprise a short amount of distraction-free time that you set aside weekly to be together as a family. They give you the opportunity to discuss values and other relevant issues, to make decisions, to problem solve, and to reinforce a sense of "family community" in an emotion-neutral zone.

Why Bother?

Initially, you might wonder what could possibly be gained from scheduling one more task into your already busy life! After all, you might think, you can make decisions and problem solve on an ad hoc basis. And clearly, you role-model values to your family daily. Why, then, should you set aside twenty to forty-five minutes of your valuable time weekly to do what you're essentially already doing?

I believe that to be truly effective parents, we must have a larger sense of purpose for everything we do. It's not enough to simply address concerns as they come up. We must also take the "long view" of parenting that we talked about in Chapter 1: asking ourselves not only, "Is what I'm doing 'working'?" (in other words, "Am I getting by?") but also, "What am I teaching to and providing for my child: am I meeting my child's needs?"

Family meetings teach our children to communicate, brainstorm, and problem solve in a group setting. In addition, they provide our children with the opportunity to contribute to something that's bigger and more important than they are. In turn, this helps them achieve a universal need of all human beings: to belong.

When our children feel as though they're making a meaningful contribution to the family "community," and when they know that the family is a place where they will *always* fit in and belong, it reduces the risk that they will reject family in favor of peer group as they grow.

> All human beings need to feel that we belong and are making a meaningful contribution to something that's bigger and more important than we are.

Making It Work

There are several guidelines that I recommend you follow to help ensure that your family meetings run smoothly. The first is to hold your family meetings on the same day and at the same time each week. This consistency is indispensable in a busy household. Without it, it's all too easy to allow something else to take priority and let family meetings go by the wayside.

Next, you need to create an agenda and post it in a convenient place where family members can write down topics they'd like to discuss or problems they'd like to brainstorm about at the next meeting. This shows your middle schooler that you're taking the idea of her contribution seriously and helps her feel integral to the family.

It's also essential to have a format for your meetings. A format keeps the goings-on orderly so that chaos doesn't ensue, with family members talking over one another so as to have their opinions heard. While any format that you might choose would probably be just fine as long as it's consistent, many families have experienced success using the following breakdown:

◄ Compliment one another. (Compliments set the tone for the meetings.)
◄ Review anything that didn't get resolved at the last meeting.
◄ Talk about new issues or decisions that need to be addressed as a family.
◄ Hand out allowances.
◄ Close the meeting with something fun—a game, a hug, ice cream . . . it can be different every time.

Use the skills of "tell me more," "listening with heart" and "cooperative communication" throughout your meetings. Remember that family meetings are supposed to help your children feel a sense of belonging. If the sessions are used for criticism and condemnation of behaviors, you won't accomplish this purpose.

The Family Meeting in Action

When Jeanne complains again about having such an early bedtime, Ruth "listens with heart" and says: "You know, I have an idea. I don't want to just arbitrarily say no to you about this, because I recognize that it's important to you. Why don't we sit down with Dad and Aaron later, and we can all discuss it?"

Later, Ruth; her husband, Dave; Jeanne; and Jeanne's nine-year-old brother, Aaron, sit down for their first family meeting.

"OK, gang," Ruth announces, "I think it's best if we have a format for our meetings so that everyone who wants to say something gets a turn. Let's start by complimenting one another. Then, if anyone has anything he or she would like to bring up, we can talk about it.

Also, I thought it would be good to give you guys your allowances during family meeting each week; that way, we won't forget to do it! What do you think?"

Aaron punches the air and exclaims, "All right, allowance!"

Jeanne sits slumped in her chair, one elbow on the table and her head in her hand. "Fine," she mutters, rolling her eyes.

Ruth wisely chooses to ignore Jeanne's body language and moves on. "OK, well, I'd like to compliment you, Dave, on finishing your big project at work." She turns to Aaron: "Aaron, I want to compliment you on working so hard on your science fair project, and Jeanne, I want to compliment you on being at this meeting even though I know you have your doubts about it." Jeanne looks uncomfortable but doesn't say anything. "Now, who'd like to go next?"

Each family member should take a turn complimenting every other family member. Starting with compliments may initially feel forced and stilted, but you'll discover that it soon becomes more natural and is often the part of the meeting to which everyone looks forward the most.

"Now," Ruth says, "does anyone have anything you'd like to talk about on the agenda today?"

"Mom," Jeanne says impatiently, "give me a break! You said we were going to have a discussion so we could talk about my bedtime, and now it's all formal and stuff. Can't we just go already?"

"I know, Jeanne," Ruth acknowledges, "and we can talk about bedtime first if you want. But I would like for us to make these discussions a habit, and I want everyone to feel included. Now, why don't you go first?"

"Mom, you *know* what I want. Come *on*!"

Jeanne's impatience is normal. Until your middle schooler realizes that these meetings can be beneficial to her, she may resist them. Be patient and persevere.

"OK, Jeanne, I know you want a later bedtime . . . "

"I want a later bedtime too!" Aaron shouts.

"Shut up," Jeanne says, glaring at him. "This isn't about you; it's about me."

"Moooommmmm!" Aaron protests.

Ruth holds up her hands. "Ground rule number one: everyone gets a chance to talk and make requests, but not all at once. If you're worried you'll forget what you want to say, write it down, but if you interrupt, your turn will be taken away. First we're going to focus on Jeanne."

"Ha!" Jeanne shouts, making a face at her brother. "OK, I don't want to go to bed so early. All my friends have a later bedtime, and you treat me like a baby."

Jeanne's father decides to use the skill of "tell me more." He asks her, "So, what time do your friends go to bed?"

Seeing a potential ally, Jeanne turns to him and replies, "Daddy, they go to bed when they want, like really late. Like 11:00. And you guys make me go to bed at 9:00, and it's just not fair."

Dave prods, "So, I'm curious as to what they're doing with that extra time?"

"Well, homework and stuff."

"So, they're using the extra time to do homework, and . . . ?"

"Well, I dunno, probably IMing or relaxing, or reading or something."

Don't rush the discussion. Slowing down will achieve more.

"What do you think you would use the extra time for?"

"I dunno. I just feel like you're treating me like a baby."

As Dave pursues a course of getting Jeanne to tell him more, Ruth is listening with heart and interjects: "So, it sounds as if you feel out of sync with your friends, as if maybe they're being treated as more grown up than you are."

"That's right, Mom, and I'm old enough too."

"Well," Dave says, "I think we can believe you're old enough to have a later bedtime. We realize that you're growing up, Jeanne. And as you continue to get older, we'll probably have to rediscuss the rules that we've set for you, so we appreciate your willingness to talk about this with us."

Ruth then engages the quality of reciprocity—acknowledging both Jeanne's need as well as Dave's and her need:

Speaking for them both, Ruth says: "We hear that you feel the need for a later bedtime. What we need is to know that you are getting enough sleep to be able to function well at school." She continues by engaging the quality of collaboration and using the skill of "cooperative communication": "What do you think we can do so that you get what you need and so that we feel reassured that you're getting enough sleep?"

Cooperative Communication:
◄ **Respect and acknowledge feelings.**
◄ **Brainstorm solutions.**
◄ **Create a plan that meets everyone's needs.**

The discussion continues, with the end result being that they will move Jeanne's bedtime incrementally and assess weekly whether her schoolwork is suffering.

The first week, they move her bedtime from 9:00 to 9:30. At the next family meeting, they agree that a 9:30 bedtime went well and they will move the bedtime again—this time to 10:00. Again, at the end of the week, it's determined that Jeanne is handling the later time well and they will try 10:30. At the following meeting, though, it's clear that 10:30 has not worked so well. Even Jeanne agrees that she feels tired in the mornings after having gone to bed so late. As a family, they decide to push Jeanne's bedtime back to 10:00 for the time being, with the provision that the discussion can be reopened at a later date by either Jeanne or her parents if things aren't going well.

Ruth and Dave do an impressive job here, allowing Jeanne to experience the natural consequences of a later bedtime and come to the decision that no matter what time her friends are going to bed, the appropriate time for her as an individual is 10:00 P.M.

Natural consequences can work in your favor.

For Jeanne, the positive outcome of getting a later bedtime reinforced the notion that family meetings weren't such a bad idea. Getting her allowance on a regular basis didn't hurt either!

Can Family Meetings Fail?

My favorite story about the challenges that can arise with family meetings was told to me by the father of three boys. They had initiated family meetings several months before, and both parents thought the meetings were going well. One day, however, only the youngest boy showed up at the appointed time. Five minutes passed; then ten. Dad began to feel annoyed. "Boys!" he shouted. "You're holding up the meeting! What's going on up there?"

"We're coming!" There was a rustling noise. Something fell, hitting the floor with a thunk. Then, silence. Another five minutes passed. Just as Dad was about to lose his cool, both boys appeared at the top of the staircase. Marching slowly down the stairs and then around the living room, each boy carried an elaborately lettered sign: "On Strike with Family Meetings!"

Family meetings rarely "fail," but sometimes they need to be adjusted so that everyone sees the benefit. If your child "goes on strike," reexamine the four qualities necessary in a relationship approach: respect, support, reciprocity, and collaboration. Put yourself in your child's shoes: If you were the child at the meeting, would you look forward to coming? Would you feel respected and supported? Would it feel as though there was a spirit of collaboration at the meeting? Would you feel listened to? Or would you worry that it was just a session in which your parents could complain about the things you were doing wrong?

The most significant outcome of any family meeting is that each child feels "heard" and respected. Even when you make a decision that your middle schooler doesn't like or agree with, if she feels that family meetings are a forum in which you "listen with heart" and she can raise issues without being criticized, she will continue to attend and be less likely to rebel.

To this end, it's best to use the first few family meetings specifically as a forum for your middle schooler and other children to voice their issues or requests. When possible, say yes or maybe to what they want, in order to reinforce the benefit of the meetings. If you must say no to a request, remember that it will elicit less rebellion if it's conditional or temporary—for example: "I'm not comfortable with that right now, but we can rediscuss it in a few weeks," or "I'm not sure I can say yes to you just yet; I'll write it down, and we'll bring it up after your next birthday." Even having to postpone a decision for a year feels less restrictive to a middle schooler than an outright "No, never!"

Finally, no one should be forced to attend family meetings. If your middle schooler chooses not to attend, have the meeting anyway—unless, of course, you're a single parent of one child. If that's the case, simply emphasize that no meeting means no allowance, since that's the time when it's handed out. Even for noncompliant middle schoolers, once they realize that nonattendance means no allowance, they'll choose to come. And once they've started to attend, they'll eventually discover that having a say in family decisions is better than having decisions made without their input.

5

Dealing with Defiance

"I lost it," Adanna says. "Asanti's attitude finally got to me, and I just couldn't keep it together."

Looking embarrassed, she continues: "I . . . stooped to her level. She was needling me since morning, and it got to be too much. I had put a nice outfit on, and the first thing out of her mouth when she saw me was, 'You're not wearing that blouse tucked in, are you? It looks terrible.'

"OK, well, I was 'good.' I let it go, and I didn't buy into her tone of voice. I said, 'Well, I'll untuck it, then.' But then it was on to the next thing. She saw that I'd fixed bacon and eggs, and she said, 'You know I don't like eggs; why do you keep fixing them?' And she took her plate and dumped the food into the trash. So, my teeth were on edge, but I still didn't react.

"Then, we were getting ready to walk out the door, and she said, 'Don't drop me off right in front of the school, Mom; you're too embarrassing.' And that was it. It was just one insult too many."

Adanna shifts uncomfortably. Looking down at her hands, she continues in a tremulous voice, "I smacked her on the arm." Her eyes well up with tears. "I've never, ever done that before. But I did. It happened so fast—like it wasn't even my own hand!"

Boy, do I feel for Adanna! I think every single one of us has been in a similar position: trying so hard to be patient and finally getting pushed to the point where we just lose it. Oh, maybe we didn't hit our child but instead grabbed her arm too tightly. Or maybe we didn't make physical contact at all but shouted or called him names. It's so hard not to lose it when a child is being as defiant as Asanti was!

The good news is that we can employ certain techniques to diminish the number of times we "lose it" with our child. Before looking at what those are, though, I want to make a couple of quick points.

First, I want to make clear that while I know everybody loses it sometimes, I do not believe that hitting our children is OK. In fact, it violates every one of the qualities we're working on during the middle school years: respect, support, reciprocity, and collaboration. All the same, I also know that sometimes we do things without thinking, things about which we later feel remorse, and we have to learn how to forgive ourselves.

FORGIVE YOURSELF

Self-forgiveness frees us to move forward and figure out productive, proactive ways to handle situations that arise in the future so that we don't repeat the behaviors we regret. It involves an admission of wrongdoing, an expression of remorse, and a desire to change.

Many people find that "confessing" what they did to a friend or another central figure in their lives creates a deeper sense of ownership than simply admitting it privately. In addition, the person in whom you confide is likely to give you feedback to reassure you that others have had similar feelings or have done something comparable. Knowing you're not the only parent in the world who's behaved in a particular way is reassuring.

Expressing remorse means apologizing when we make a mistake. Some parents find this extremely difficult, especially when, as in Adanna's case, they sincerely felt that the child had "crossed the line" and pushed them to the point of losing control. Apologizing to your child does *not* excuse the child's bad behavior, which you will handle separately. It simply frees you from your own feelings of anger and guilt so that you can more effectively deal with your middle schooler's attitude or actions.

> Forgiving yourself is the first step in
> not making the mistake a second time.

Finally, a desire to change will allow you to seek out other ways of managing similar situations in the future. It doesn't guarantee that you'll never lose it again (after all, we're all human!), but it does create a foundation on which you can become a better parent.

Once you're on the road to forgiveness (you don't have to be all the way there yet), it's time to take a look at ways to do things differently next time. The next step, and one that I believe is crucial, is to attempt to figure out why in the world your middle schooler is being so defiant.

UNDERSTANDING YOUR MIDDLE SCHOOLER'S BEHAVIOR

For some middle schoolers, the discomfort associated with this developmental stage is overwhelming. While all middle schoolers are porcupines some of the time, for others it is a stage in which their quills are perpetually on guard as if the world is a predator and they must keep everyone at bay. Often, this manifests itself in an intensely defiant attitude, such that even the most calm parent would be challenged.

When our middle schooler has his quills out for attack, it's helpful to see if we can determine why he is behaving this way. Keep in mind that if we find an explanation for his actions, it does not mean we will *excuse* the behavior. Our goal when we look for an explanation is simply to help us decide what technique might be the most effective in the particular situation.

Also, it may be, in the end, that we simply can't figure out a specific cause for his behavior, and that's OK. Rather, we may have to fall back on the truth that for many middle schoolers, defiance and anger are ways in which they keep the world at arm's length during their metamorphosis so they won't get hurt. In addition, many pre-teens and teens struggle with how to effectively separate from their parents. Subconsciously, some believe that if they're nasty enough, it will push their parents away, making the process of becoming independent easier.

> Explaining behavior does *not* mean
> excusing behavior.

Still, looking for an explanation is a worthwhile exercise. Not only will it give us further insight into our middle schooler's metamorphosis, but it stands to help us build a strong, empathetic relationship with her as well.

The Four Goals of Misbehavior

For the moment, let's set aside the relatively universal reasons that middle schoolers act in defiant ways and take a look at some specific, subconscious reasons that might cause them to behave in a particular manner.

In *Children: The Challenge*, the renowned educator Rudolf Dreikers proposed four principal reasons why children misbehave: they want attention, they want power, they want revenge, or they are feeling inadequate. If we can identify our middle schooler's explicit goal, we can be careful not to unintentionally reward bad behavior by giving her what she wants. Likewise, we can help her achieve her goal in more positive ways. Keep in mind that these goals are subconscious and that you should not expressly identify or articulate them to your middle schooler.

◅ **Seeking attention.** All human beings want and need attention. If your middle schooler is feeling left out, lonely, or ignored, he may try to draw attention to himself by being rude or engaging in other misbehaviors that elicit your attention.

◅ **Seeking power or control.** Preadolescents, who are neither child nor teen, often feel out of control and powerless. Some of their behavior may be directed toward the goal of gaining power. This can take the form of language, such as using four-letter words or arguing with you. It can also be behavioral. Remember Uma, the child from Chapter 1 who didn't call her mother when she got to her gymnastics class? Her behavior is a prime example of a child seeking power and control by grabbing more independence than Mom had offered.

◅ **Seeking revenge.** When a child is feeling hurt by something that someone did or said (*or by what he perceives was done or said to him*), he may desire to hurt back in the form of revenge. Revenge can be active or passive. Active revenge might take the form of words meant to hurt you, such as Asanti's saying that her mother was "embarrassing," or behaviors that are blatantly rude, such as Asanti's throwing her breakfast in the trash. Passive revenge might take the form of "forgetting" to do a chore and thereby inconveniencing you or the rest of the family, such as not taking out the trash when you had fish that night.

◄ **Seeking withdrawal.** The desire to withdraw comes from a sense of inadequacy or a fear of failure. Remember Jordan, our overwhelmed slacker from Chapter 2? His fear of failure and sense of inadequacy caused him to withdraw by shoving his books under his bed and ignoring his homework.

Asanti's Goal

Looking back at the situation between Adanna and Asanti, we can see that Asanti is acting in vengeful ways. Her mother's hurt feelings underscore the possibility that for some reason, Asanti is "seeking revenge." Note that a child needn't have actually been hurt to seek revenge. She can also seek revenge for an *imagined* hurt—for example, if, without knowing it, we said or did something that accidentally "shook the chrysalis."

Another possibility, though, is that Asanti is feeling hurt by the world right now and is taking it out on her mother. Sometimes middle schoolers still believe that their parents can fix things, and when the parent doesn't read the child's mind and do so, the response is to feel angry and vengeful. The question is: Did anything happen in school or with Asanti's friends that might cause her to feel hurt and lash out in the way that she's doing?

When Adanna hears this question, her eyes widen with recognition. "I forgot," she blurts, "she auditioned for the school play just last week, and she found out yesterday that she didn't get in. She told me that the girl who got the lead is the girlfriend of the student director, and that's why she got the part instead of Asanti. I forgot all about that. Maybe that's why she's feeling so hurt!"

Adanna is probably right, although, as we've seen, this isn't the first time Asanti has exhibited a defiant attitude. Sometimes our child's behavior is an isolated incident in which we can figure out what's bothering her at the moment. Other times, though, her behavior is part of a larger pattern. In either case, however, it's useful to choose one instance of misbehavior to analyze. Then, we can slowly zoom out to look at the larger picture and see if we can discover a pattern of similar goals that is causing our middle schooler to behave in a particular way.

How Adanna's Response Played a Role

In addition to hypothesizing about what our middle schooler's goal might be, it's advantageous to look more closely at how we communicate with our preteen. For an illustration of the role that communication plays in our children's behavior, let's look in on how Adanna responded when Asanti told her that she hadn't made the school play.

Adanna relates: "Well, I told her that these things happen sometimes. It's not right, but politics and favoritism play a part when you're in the theater or anywhere else. I said that she should learn to expect this kind of thing if she wants to be an actress."

Here is an unfortunate example of good intentions combined with poor communication. Although Adanna wants to soothe Asanti's hurt feelings about not being cast in the play, she has unintentionally sent a pretty unsympathetic message.

Remember our discussion in Chapter 3 of what we say versus what our middle schooler hears? The same thing is happening in this instance. Adanna means to tell Asanti that she's talented but that favoritism sometimes means an untalented actress might get a part for which Asanti is actually better suited. Unfortunately, what Asanti *hears* her mother saying is probably something more like: "Quit whining about it. You'd better toughen up if you want to do this acting thing." During a time when Asanti needs for her mother to respond to her hurt feelings and commiserate, she feels put off, more hurt, and misunderstood. This can lead to vengeful actions.

I want to underscore a fundamental point at this time: in *no way* am I blaming Adanna for her daughter's appalling behavior. It's not Adanna's fault that Asanti was rude, lashed out, and threw her breakfast into the garbage. Asanti bears *full* responsibility for these actions.

Seeking to understand her behavior is not an end unto itself. Rather, it provides a means for us to develop a strategy. If we're able to ascertain all of the contributing factors, such as the way in which we might be sending the wrong message to our middle schooler, we may be able to break out of a negative think-feel-do cycle.

> Understanding our middle schooler does *not* mean we are condoning misbehavior or rudeness.

COMMUNICATION BLOCKS

Unbeknownst to Adanna, she has inadvertently engaged in what we call "communication blocks." Michael Popkin, author of the video-based parenting-education program *Active Parenting*, names nine ways that parents miscommunicate with their children when the child is having a problem:

Communication block	How it sounds	What your middle schooler thinks when he hears you say it
Commanding	"Quit whining." "Stop complaining." "Calm down."	"What I have to say is unimportant." "I don't count."
Advising	"Next time, you should . . ." "Well, what you need to do is go back to her and explain that . . ."	"I never do anything right." "What happens is all my fault."
Placating	"Oh, honey. You're beautiful/talented/ smart no matter what she/he said about you."	"Mom/Dad doesn't understand me." "Mom/Dad is lying."

Communication block	How it sounds	What your middle schooler thinks when he hears you say it
Distracting	"You know what: let's go out to lunch to take your mind off of it."	"Feelings are bad." "I need to bury my feelings or distract myself from them."
Interrogating	"Well, what did you do to make him say that?"	"If something bad happens, it must be because I did something wrong."
Moralizing	"Every cloud has a silver lining." "Tomorrow's a new day; it will be better then."	"My feelings don't count except as a way for Mom/ Dad to prove a bigger lesson about life."
Psychologizing	"How do you feel about that? And why do you feel that way?"	"No one else feels this way: I need to explain my feelings because they're so unusual."
Using sarcasm	"It's not the end of the world, after all, you know."	"I'm a jerk/stupid for having feelings about this."
Being a know-it-all	"Honey, that's just the way these things go. You have to chalk this one up to the law of averages. By the time you're twenty . . . (blah, blah, blah)."	"I'm not allowed to feel the way I feel because there's always a bigger explanation that makes more sense than what I think or feel."

When most parents hear about these communication blocks, they think: "Wait a sec—I say those things all the time! If I can't use those, I'm never going to be able to speak to my child again!"

Feeling overwhelmed by the number of ways we can *mis*communicate with our middle schooler is normal. All of a sudden, the way we've been communicating with him throughout elementary school has to be discarded. But wait! Before you throw this book down and run screaming from the room, I want to give you what I call my "70-30 rule": You have to "get it right" only 70 percent of the time. That leaves a 30 percent margin for error.

No one has to be perfect. No one can be perfect. The 70-30 rule gives us a percentage with which most of us can live. It allows for forgiveness of self, even when you "lose it" as Adanna did. It also gives us permission to "not get it right" a decent amount of the time, while still giving us a reasonable standard to live up to. So, if you block communication, especially as you're still learning these new skills, that's OK. Recognizing our contribution to these negative cycles is half the battle—even if it occurs after the fact.

THE DANCE OF DEFIANCE

Now we understand the possible "why" of Asanti's behavior, at least in this instance: she was upset about not getting into the play and felt unfairly treated. Adanna's "logical" response inadvertently caused Asanti to feel misunderstood and hurt, which, in turn, led to her vengeful behavior. Zooming out now to look at the bigger picture, we can also assume that there may be a pattern between Adanna and Asanti of blocked communication, resulting in Asanti's ongoing defiant behavior.

Cue the Orchestra

Let's envision the way in which we communicate and otherwise engage with our middle schoolers as a dance. Imagine a large ballroom, with beautiful music playing. Assume that you're an experienced ballroom dancer. You and your partner (in this case, your middle schooler) are dancing to the music, but he keeps stepping on your toes. Understandably, this annoys you, but you have hope that he will improve, so you keep dancing. And it happens again. And again. Now your toes are getting sore, and you're more than annoyed:

you're downright angry! How dare he? It's not *your* fault, since you're the more experienced of the two. Why does he keep hurting you and messing up the dance?

Now imagine a different scenario. You're still in a ballroom, and again you're dancing with your middle school "partner." He steps on your toes the first time, and you keep dancing. But the second time, or maybe the third, you stop dancing; you drop his hand and just stand there. You have now disengaged from the dance. This is not because you were doing something wrong—in fact, quite the opposite, since you were the experienced dancer, as we know. Regardless, when you take the initiative and disengage, the dance simply cannot continue, because your middle schooler no longer has anyone with whom to perform the steps.

Disengaging from the Dance

Disengaging from the dance can be done in several ways: by mentally disengaging, by using a "parental time-out," or by inserting a technique into the "do" part of the think-feel-do cycle that we talked about in Chapter 2. It can also be done proactively, by avoiding communication blocks and "listening with heart." Let's examine each of these separately.

Mentally Disengaging. Adanna tried hard to mentally disengage from the dance by letting Asanti's first two outbursts slide. Sometimes this is an effective method—what one of my experienced group members and the parent of two middle schoolers calls "Zen parenting." You take a deep breath, you pretend you didn't hear your middle schooler, you move on, and later you complain about it to a friend.

This particular technique can also be described as "taking down the sails." If you were in a sailboat, and a terrible wind came up, the best way to protect yourself would be to fold up the sails. If the wind has nothing to blow against, the boat isn't going to capsize. However, there are times when this method isn't effective. In Adanna's case, she wasn't able to take down the sails fully. Over time, Asanti's tempest was strong enough to push her mother's boat over.

> **Mentally disengage only once.**
> **If it doesn't break you out of the dance,**
> **choose a different method.**

Mental disengagement is best used in single-instance circumstances. The first time your child "steps on your foot" in the dance, you can mentally disengage. If the behavior doesn't come back, great. But if the behavior does recur, it's time to try something else. We don't want Zen parenting to turn into denial.

Parental Time-Out. Sometimes we need to physically disengage— to take what I call a "parental time-out." Parental time-outs are an incredibly effective tool for handling middle schoolers, particularly when you feel your anger building, as Adanna did. In her situation, a parental time-out might have been used in the following way:

After Asanti dumped her food into the trash, Adanna could have said: "Asanti, what's happening this morning is not good for our relationship. I'm going into the other room until I calm down." Then, Adanna could have left the room and taken as much time as she needed to pull herself together. If that meant that Asanti was late for school, then Asanti would experience the natural consequences of her defiant behavior.

Inserting a Technique. We've already looked at a number of techniques in previous chapters that could be inserted to change the steps of the dance. One such technique is the "I statement," which can be used separately from "sandwiching." It might sound like this: "Asanti, I'm angry and hurt"; or, "I feel picked on and unappreciated." When we use an "I statement" in this way, we can go one step further and "tag it" with either a limit or a consequence.

Limits are statements that define the rules.
Consequences are the logical actions you take
when your middle schooler breaks a rule.

◄ **Tagging the "I statement" with a limit.** Tagging the "I statement" with a limit might sound like this: ["**I statement**"] "I'm angry and hurt. [**Limit**] I want you to refrain from commenting about the way I dress and the way I cook."

When we tag the "I statement" with a limit, it's tempting to try to drive the point home by using too many words. Wordiness will only make your middle schooler tune you out. You have only a small window of opportunity for her to hear you; use it efficiently. Less is more!

◄ **Tagging the "I statement" with a consequence.** Tagging the "I statement" with a consequence might sound like this: ["**I statement**"] "I feel picked on and unappreciated. [**Consequence**] Tomorrow you can cook your own breakfast."

Note that the consequence must be logically related to Asanti's behavior—in this case, throwing her breakfast into the garbage. Creating consequences that are logically related is essential to breaking out of the dance of defiance.

To contrast this example of a "logical" consequence with one that illustrates an "illogical" consequence, consider the perennial favorite "You're grounded." Keeping your middle schooler home for throwing her breakfast into the garbage isn't related to the behavior. It's illogical. While imposing such a consequence might give you an immediate sense of power and control, I promise it will be short lived. The less logical the consequence, the more likely your middle schooler is to feel hurt and seek revenge, which will only perpetuate the cycle.

A PROACTIVE APPROACH: DON'T DANCE TO BEGIN WITH

Because Asanti has been consistently defiant, it's helpful to also consider a long-term, proactive approach. In other words, how can Adanna avoid the dance, even if she doesn't know she's on the dance floor?

The most effective method requires first being aware of the communication blocks that we use the most often. For example, I know that I have several weak areas in this regard: I love to offer advice (no surprise there, given that I write books full of advice!), and I'm also so empathetic that when my children are upset, I want to soothe their hurt feelings. This makes me more likely to block communication through placating and distracting.

Like a good coach who reviews the tape from last night's football game in an effort to improve the next game, let's rewind "our" tape and analyze the communication blocks that Adanna could have avoided when Asanti told her that she didn't make the school play:

- ◄ "Well, I told her that these things happen sometimes." (Moralizing)
- ◄ "It's not right, but politics and favoritism play a part when you're in the theater or anywhere else." (Being a know-it-all)
- ◄ "I said that she should learn to expect this kind of thing if she wants to be an actress." (Giving advice)

Looks as if Adanna was "0 for 3!"

SO, NOW WHAT? APPLYING WHAT WE'VE LEARNED

As we continued our conversation, Adanna realized that she would often respond with one of these three communication blocks when Asanti was upset. In recognizing this, Adanna has already freed herself to respond differently in the future. The question is: What kind of response can Adanna make that won't unwittingly engage her in another dance?

Once we're aware of our "favorite" ways of blocking communication when our child is expressing his feelings, we can consciously work to avoid responding in those ways. However, as we know, nature abhors a vacuum, and if we simply try to keep our mouths shut and not respond at all, we might eventually be goaded into it. So, rather than have a void in which we're just staring blankly at our middle schooler, we can "listen with heart," the skill we learned in Chapter 1.

Once More with Feeling

In Adanna's case, she could have employed this skill when Asanti told her about not being cast in the school production. Let's eavesdrop on an imaginary conversation to see how it might play out:

Asanti slams into the house. "I'm so furious! I didn't get the part."

Seeing the look of anger on Asanti's face, Adanna says, "Oh no! Asanti, you must feel so disappointed!"

"Mom, Rose is a terrible actress; she just got the part because she's John's girlfriend."

Listening does not equal coddling.

"John's girlfriend? That's infuriating—that kind of political game just makes my skin crawl. And you're such a good actress too. This is totally unfair."

In this conversation, Mom is listening and empathizing. Sometimes parents worry that empathy will make things worse rather than better, but that's rarely the case. When children feel understood, it provides relief from the negative feelings they're having.

While it doesn't show up here, you should be prepared for a middle schooler who is feeling intensely angry to experiment with using curse words. When they do, it will be tempting to address the foul language at the moment that it occurs, but keep in mind that there is value in waiting. Correcting offensive speech in the middle of a rant by your preteen will only block communication and make things worse. Instead, choose a neutral time and place to set limits about language, such as a family meeting.

Timing is important.

Cooperative Communication

Let's look at another example of middle school defiance. The middle child in her family, Hannah has always felt competitive with her older sister, Caley, whom we met in Chapter 4 and who is only one year ahead of her in school. Although Hannah is not a bad student, academics don't come as easily to her as they do to her big sister. It was a Saturday afternoon, and Hannah had a project due for school on Monday. Her mother, Dahlia, gently reminded her that she might want to get started, and Hannah exploded! She stormed off to her room, slammed the door, and shouted that she was never coming out.

In this situation, we might guess that Hannah is "seeking withdrawal." Perhaps she is worried about failing, not living up to her own expectations or to the expectations of others. Let's listen to how Dahlia handles the situation:

"First," Dahlia recounts, "I didn't barge into her room like I used to. I just gave her some space."

This is a nice tactic. Not only does it respect Hannah's need to withdraw, but also it gives Dahlia an opportunity to think about how she might handle the situation. If Mom had dashed into Hannah's room, she might have been tempted to try to bolster her confidence, give advice, or engage in any of a number of other communication blocks. By restraining this impulse (one that most parents might experience), she doesn't give either of them the opportunity to engage in the dance of defiance.

Dahlia continues: "So, Hannah goes into her room, and the minutes started ticking away. I keep looking at the clock. All I can think about is how long the project will take and how much time is being wasted. After an hour, I'm really nervous, and it takes everything I have not to go in there. But I don't. When she finally comes out, I just touch her shoulder and say, 'Hey. Can I help?' "

Hannah then responds: "No. Nobody can. I'll never be a good student, never!"

"Sounds as if you're pretty discouraged right now," Dahlia says. Her tone is empathetic. "This project seems to be getting you down, huh?"

"I'll never get it done."

"You sound really overwhelmed. Is there anything you can think of that would make this feel more manageable?"

Hannah's eyes fill with tears as she looks away. "No."

Dahlia asks, "Well, Hannah, do you think it would help if you broke it down into smaller tasks?"

"Mom, nothing will help. I'm going to get an F," Hannah asserts.

"Would you feel less overwhelmed and more encouraged if you had someone with you in the room when you started working on it?"

Hannah's shoulders droop. "No one's gonna do that."

Dahlia replies, "I will."

"You will?" Hannah asks, surprised. "But you have so many other things you need to do. You don't have time to just sit with me while I do my homework."

Hannah is using a fairly sophisticated "withdrawal technique" here. She's clearly intrigued with the idea of having Dahlia sit with her, but she may be reluctant to give up her avoidance behavior. Thus, she tries to convince Dahlia that Mom doesn't really mean what she's offered. At this point, it would be tempting for Dahlia to become overly enthusiastic and say something like: "It's not a problem at all! Let's get your poster board. Here, I'll sharpen some pencils, you go get the notes you took, and we'll have this done in no time!" However, if Dahlia moves into "fix-it" mode, it will only add to Hannah's sense that she can't do it on her own.

"I know I have other things to do," Dahlia tells her. "I also know that it sometimes helps to have someone with you if you're feeling overwhelmed. What do you think?"

"Well, OK," Hannah says.

Looking at What Went Right. Dahlia did a beautiful job in this interaction with Hannah, moving her from discouraged to motivated by using the skill of "cooperative communication." Let's look at her success step by step.

As I mentioned before, the first thing Dahlia did well was to stay out of Hannah's way by not barging in to her room. In their book *Raising a Daughter: Parents and the Awakening of a Healthy Woman*, Jeanne and Don Elium present the "Bell Curve of Feelings":

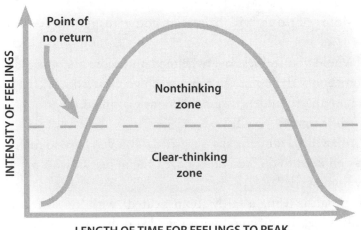

LENGTH OF TIME FOR FEELINGS TO PEAK
AND THEN RETURN TO NEUTRAL

Looking at the chart, we can see that Hannah had reached the "point of no return" and was clearly in the "nonthinking zone." Allowing time for her feelings to recede was an excellent idea.

Once Hannah emerged from her room, Dahlia "listened with heart": "Sounds as if you're pretty discouraged right now." Acknowledging her discouragement helped Hannah feel understood by her mother, which, in turn, opened her to hearing whatever else her mother might want to say.

Next, Dahlia moved into brainstorming solutions: " . . . do you think it would help if you . . . " Using questions rather than statements created a collaborative atmosphere and allowed Dahlia to avoid blocking communication by giving advice. However, Hannah's desire for withdrawal was appreciable, which threw a roadblock into their conversation. Dahlia remained undaunted, though, and continued communicating until a solution was reached.

Give Yourself Credit. I told Dahlia how well I thought she'd handled this situation, but upon receiving the compliment, she looked embarrassed and said, "I don't know—maybe it was just coincidence. I mean, maybe if I hadn't done any of that, she would have come around anyway."

All too often, parents are willing to take blame for a slew of negative occurrences but are not so willing to give themselves credit for the positive outcomes. That's a shame. It's only through recognizing the payoffs of our hard work that we're motivated to keep working. If we can congratulate ourselves for a job well done, we will have begun the path to many more successes in the future.

> **The hard work of learning and using these techniques deserves praise!**

6

The Computer "Addiction"

"I'm having a problem with Martin's computer use," Gary begins, "and it's also affecting Jeremy and Cheryl." Gary is the father of Martin (age twelve), Jeremy (age ten), and Cheryl (age eight). The epitome of an involved and caring dad, he has attended parenting groups with me since his oldest was a toddler.

"All of them seem addicted in some way," he continues. "Martin is into those role-playing games. If I ask him to get off the computer, he says, 'One more minute, Dad; I just have to finish this quest.' Jeremy plays the online arcade-type games, so he always says, 'I just have to finish this level.' And Cheryl has already figured out how to instant-message her friends, which is distracting her from homework and chores." He pauses to look at me and then asks seriously, "Do you think they're addicted?"

COMPUTER ADDICTION: REALITY OR MYTH?

When children spend a lot of time online or playing video games, it can certainly seem as though they're addicted! But are they really? The jury's still out, but it's worthwhile to note that in 2007, the American Medical Association reported that approximately 90 percent of American youths play video games on their computers and handheld devices. In addition, the researchers proposed that approximately 15 percent of them *might* be addicted. The AMA stopped short of classifying video game overuse as an addiction but did urge further research. And a 2007 report by the Council on Science and Public Health found that overuse of video games had similar patterns of behavior to other addictive disorders.

Of course, video games, CRPGs (computer role-playing games), and MMORPGs (massive multiplayer online role-playing games) are not the only attraction that can preoccupy our children on the computer. They share the field with television and video (now readily available online), instant messaging, e-mailing, visiting websites, and "hanging out" in areas such as MySpace and Facebook. There are also more educationally oriented activities, such as word processing, blogging, researching, and reading.

For Gary, and for the rest of us, concern about our middle schoolers' use of computers should focus both on safety and on whether computer use interferes with other healthy activities. To determine the latter, ask yourself the following questions:

- ◄ Does my child play on the computer to the exclusion of other pleasurable activities, such as time with family or friends, exercise, being outside, or extracurricular activities?
- ◄ Does my child forget to eat regular meals because of computer use?
- ◄ Does my child stay up past bedtime to finish activities other than homework on the computer?
- ◄ Does my child use stimulants (such as Coca-Cola, Red Bull, coffee, or tea) to stay awake longer in order to continue to use the computer?

◄ Does my child seem overly anxious to get back to the computer when asked to do something else for a while?

◄ Does my child appear to be cranky, fidgety, or ill at ease when engaged in activities other than the computer?

◄ Have my child's grades been suffering recently?

◄ Is my child on the computer for reasons other than homework more than one to two hours a day? (This is the 2007 American Academy of Pediatrics recommended guideline for daily on-screen time.)

Before you begin a conversation with your middle schooler about the amount of time he spends on the computer, it's beneficial to have some information about what he's actually doing when he is online.

STAYING INFORMED

Because of rapidly changing technology, staying informed is both the most difficult and the most necessary task we face in helping our children remain psychologically healthy and physically safe. Here's a short "crash course" in current technology. Bear in mind that as our children grow, it's important to talk to other parents, go online ourselves, and ask our children questions to keep abreast of technological changes.

Video Games

Video games can be played at an arcade or on a personal computer, television set (with the purchase of extra hardware such as Sony PlayStation, Xbox, or Wii), handheld device (such as Game Boy), cell phone, or PDA (personal digital assistant). Many of these games do not have to be purchased; they can be downloaded or played on the Web for free. These "free" Web games are usually accompanied by banner advertising. According to answers.com, games fall within six categories: fighting; shooting; strategy; simulations; adventure; and run, jump, and avoid (RJA).

CRPGs: Computer Role-Playing Games

Answers.com describes computer role-playing games as ones in which the user creates a character (such as a wizard) that can move freely throughout a graphic fantasy environment online. CRPGs are typically social and collaborative rather than competitive. Many people from all over the world can play and communicate at the same time, within certain prescribed rules. Because the games are episodic in nature, they may go on for weeks, months, and even years.

MMORPGs: Massive Multiplayer Online Role-Playing Games

On Wisegeek.com, Michael Anissimov explains that massive multiplayer online role-playing games are distinguished from CRPGs by the large number of people (in the thousands) who can play at one time. Most have a theme, including fantasy, sword and sorcery, crime fiction, science fiction, or the occult. If your middle schooler plays these games, you may hear him talking about "quests," "monsters," and "loot." MMORPGs always allow communication between players. In fact, according to wikipedia.org, players are often expected to join some type of group or team, such as a "guild" within which they will be asked to play a certain role—"healer," for instance. It is often possible for players to purchase (with real money) intriguing or necessary items for their characters. This is usually done through PayPal, using a parent's credit card.

IMing: Instant Messaging

Instant messaging allows our middle schoolers to communicate with one another over the Internet in "real time." Instant messages are text based and often use abbreviated spellings to speed the process. Webopedia.com lists more than five hundred recognized abbreviations. A few examples are ttyl (talk to you later), pos (parent over shoulder), kotl (kiss on the lips), and kpc (keeping parents clueless). Typically, users of IM create a private list of people who are allowed to chat with them. The instant messaging system alerts the user when someone on the person's private list is online.

Social Networking Websites

The National Institute on Media and the Family calls social networking websites "the modern day version of the corner drug-store where kids go to socialize, express themselves, and hang out." A person's "page" is also called a "profile" and has been compared to a virtual bedroom that can be redecorated and personalized with graphics, photos, videos, and blogs by and blurbs about the person. Detailed personal information may also be included, such as name, age, residence, and school. In his article "MySpace and Your Kids," Dr. David Walsh says that social networking sites allow youths to "try out new identities and looks, express themselves in new ways, and socialize." Examples of this type of site include MySpace, Facebook, and Friendster.

Web Surfing

Surfing the Web can consume hours of a middle schooler's time. Some websites are, of course, educational; others are entertaining; still others are pornographic. There are even search engines that will surf the Web on your behalf, selecting sites you might enjoy based on those you've been to in the past.

Blogging

A blog is similar to a personal diary kept online that can be viewed by others. Some blogs also contain pictures and links to other websites.

KEEPING OUR KIDS SAFE

Honestly, just contemplating the vast number of ways in which our middle schooler can be involved online often feels imposing and maybe even horrifying. And concern about the Internet is, quite frankly, warranted. Our children often equate sitting in the privacy of one's own home with being safe, yet the reality is the opposite. Considering that anything posted on the Web or communicated over the Internet is "public information," if your middle schooler has a profile on MySpace, is IMing, or even is e-mailing, it's possible for him to communicate with strangers, and strangers may initiate conversations with him.

While both hardware and software solutions are available for keeping kids safe on the Internet, rapidly changing technology precludes listing them, because they'd likely be outdated with the next advancement. There are solutions, however, that will never be obsolete—ones that have to do with your relationship and communicating with your middle schooler.

Strategies for Staying Informed

Among the most highly regarded techniques you can develop in order to remain informed about your middle schooler's computer use are the skills of "listening with heart" and "tell me more." When we ask our preteens about the activities in which they've exhibited interest, when we're curious about how their world "works," and when we refrain from a judgmental attitude as we listen, we create an environment in which they're more likely to share information with us.

With regard to computer activities, "listening" and showing interest involve more than just asking them questions at dinnertime. In fact, the most effective way to listen with heart in this case is to actually sit with your child while he plays an MMORPG, watches a You Tube video, or participates in an online video arcade game. Some parents are dismayed when they hear this advice, and you might be too. You might think: "Arrghh! That's torture! I couldn't care less about 'loot' and 'advancing' and that role-playing stuff. I hate that kind of thing; it's so boring!"

I understand, believe me. It can feel torturous to passively watch your child play a game or to attempt to discern what she finds hilarious about a three-minute amateur video she's discovered. But "acting as if" we're interested in our children's lives—including their online lives—undeniably strengthens the bonds of our relationship with our middle schooler as almost nothing else can.

"Act As If." The American psychologist and philosopher William James (1842–1910) said, "If you want a quality, act as if you already had it." For parents, this means that if we "act as if" we're interested in what our middle schooler cares about, we will actually *become* interested. And having an interest in their activities—online and off—is the means to maintaining both a relationship and open lines of communication.

"Acting as if" carries a lot of benefits, some that you might find surprising. For example, Ruth found that acting interested in Jeanne's IMing led to increased communication and expressions of tenderness in their household. At night, if everyone was busy doing homework or other things on the computer, Jeanne might send a quick IM to her mom or dad just saying, "I love you," to which Ruth or Dave would respond, "You're the best!"

Similarly, Gary noticed that while he'd always been interested in his son Jeremy's arcade games, he hadn't paid much attention to the online activities of Martin or Cheryl. He noted that he'd felt closer to Jeremy than the other two until he began to make an effort to show interest in their online activities and games. In addition, he found that "hanging out" with them while they were on the computer gave him access to information about what they were doing that he wouldn't have otherwise gleaned.

> "Acting as if" is one of the best tools to stay
> informed about our children's online activities.

Engaging the Help of Others. Another invaluable strategy lies in engaging the help of other parents in our network. Talking with others allows us to be aware of websites, games, or even dangers we might not have known about, and it arms us with information about what other parents allow their children to do, or where they allow their children to go online. Having this information doesn't mean that we must bend our own rules or change our values if they're different from someone else's, but it does broaden our perspective and give us a sense of what other middle schoolers are doing.

Strategies for Communicating Limits or Concerns

"OK," says Samantha, "let's say I act as if I'm interested in Nicholas's game thing. I still don't want him to spend all that time on the computer. His schoolwork has been fine so far, but he'll be in high school next year, and I'm worried that his game will take precedence."

There's no question that a computer game and homework or chores should have different levels of priority. However, we still have to consider the most effective way to set limits on our children's computer activities. Finding out more about what your child is doing on the computer and respecting his interest in it will actually give you a stronger base for voicing your concerns.

Remember that because of his developmental level, his priorities are going to be different from yours. When he's engaged in a "quest," it feels just as important to him as finishing an assignment before its deadline does to you. If you insist that your son turn off his game right away when he's in the middle of something, in his eyes you may be ruining a lot of "work" that he's done. Now, you and I both know that it's not really work, but respecting our children's needs or interests means that if your child *thinks* it's important, then it's tantamount to *being* important. Recognizing that their priorities are different from ours because of their developmental level helps us engage the qualities of reciprocity and collaboration.

Framing Limits. Once you're familiar with your child's online preferences, you will be able to empathetically set limits on computer use. For example, Gary might be concerned that Martin is delaying his chores in favor of playing on the computer. To communicate this concern to his son, he might say: "Martin, I know that you need to act as healer for your guild right now and that they're counting on you. I need to make sure the chores get done before 7:00. How can we work this out?"

Using Reciprocity + Collaboration to Set Limits:
◄ "I know you need _____."
◄ "What I need is _____."
◄ "How can we work this out?"

While this may sound as though Gary is coddling Martin, what he's effectively doing is stepping into Martin's world and building a bridge between that world and his own. In using Martin's player lingo, he's recognizing his son's developmental need to be connected to his peers—albeit through a game on the Web.

Now, if Gary were simply to barge in and say: "Enough of that game thing. Get off right now. There are more important things that have to get done around here," he would essentially be lobbing a hand grenade across the gap that exists between middle schooler and adult and would destroy his bridge-building chance.

Of course, if Martin ignores Gary and does not complete the chores by 7:00, then Gary would give Martin a consequence: shortening his computer time the next day, for example, or telling him that *when* he's finished the chores, *then* he can play on the computer.

Using a "when/then" structure in our language
helps our middle schoolers manage their time
with a "work first, play later" philosophy.

Some parents argue that the empathetic approach of setting limits won't penetrate when their middle schooler is engrossed in computer activities. For instance, Samantha argues that if she were to engage reciprocity and collaboration with Nicholas, he would probably just grunt or make promises he wouldn't keep. If this is the case with your child, you could try setting limits using a more proactive approach such as the "sandwich technique" introduced in Chapter 3.

Using the Sandwich Technique. Let's say that Samantha feels that Nick's immersion in his MMORPG is interfering with time that he could be using to get a project done. Acting proactively, Samantha should start by scripting herself. Then, she can choose a time when Nick is not playing his game on the computer to put her script into action.

For example, she might say: "How's your quest coming, Nick? Did you advance a level yet?" This initial statement, using "tell me more," is a way of introducing the topic you ultimately want to talk about.

After "listening with heart," Samantha could say: [**Bread**] "It sounds as if you're making some real progress there and you've been an asset to your guild. I enjoy hearing about your new exploits! [**Meat**] I feel somewhat concerned that you were up so late last night and that it might be a squeeze to get your science project done in time if you don't work on it pretty faithfully. [**Bread**] I'm sure you've thought about how to balance this, though. Why don't you tell me what your plan is?"

Remember: It's tempting to join the bread to
the meat with "but." Refrain from doing so!

By using the skill of "exhibiting trust" that we learned in Chapter 3 and communicating her belief that Nick already has a plan for creating balance between his online community and his schoolwork, Samantha puts forth a positive expectation. As we know, children often live up to our expectations. Thus, articulating those expectations is crucial.

The Trust Contract. But what happens if Nick doesn't respond positively to Samantha's "sandwich" approach? If that's the case, she can then set up a "trust contract" by coming up with a consequence and a way for him to earn back her trust. She might tell him that his time on the computer will be strictly supervised for a week and that he can have only a half hour per day. If he proves that he can be trusted to turn off the computer after half an hour each day during that period, then he'll earn more time. If he can't be responsible and turn it off, he'll get less time.

COMPUTER USE AND PERSONAL SAFETY

Our children's safety is another area in which we must be both informed and vigilant. How can we ensure that they're safe from strangers when they're on the Web? Let's take a look at some facts regarding predation on the Internet, and then we'll talk about how to communicate these facts to our middle schoolers.

Is Your Child at Risk?

According to Michael Ryan, owner of PC Sentinel Software, most victims of Internet crime are between twelve and fifteen years old. They use instant messaging but have not set their IM account to block strangers. They can be either naive or the opposite—willing to take serious risks. These children are often secretive about their online activities, have few interests outside of the Internet, and spend more than ninety minutes per day of nonhomework time on the computer.

They frequently believe they are talking to someone their own age online. Victims often live in suburban or rural towns and tend not to have many off-line friends.

The danger of our middle schooler's being in contact with a stranger online is that a predator can encourage or manipulate our child into revealing personal information that will lead the predator to where our child lives or goes to school. The predator may urge our child to meet somewhere. Because most kids believe they're speaking to a peer rather than an adult, they are not alerted to the potential danger until it's too late. In addition, some predators persuade children to view pornography or to send them nude or partially dressed photos or videos of themselves online.

Is Your Child in Contact with a Predator?

According to the attorney general's office, one in five children who use a computer is sexually solicited online, and only 25 percent tell their parents. The FBI names seven warning signs that your child may be in contact with a predator. Ask yourself the following questions:

- ◄ Is my middle schooler making calls to numbers I don't recognize? Has a man whom I don't know called the house asking to speak to my child? (Nearly 100 percent of all sexual abuse is committed by heterosexual males, but you should be wary of *anyone* whom you don't know who's contacting your child.)
- ◄ Has my child received gifts, packages, or letters from unknown sources? Predators often seduce children by sending gifts to create a sense of being cared for.
- ◄ Does my child seem secretive in his computer use? Does he turn off the monitor or change the screen when I walk into the room?
- ◄ Does my child spend large amounts of time on the computer, especially at night?

◄ Is there pornography on my child's computer? Has my child visited pornographic sites?

◄ Does my middle schooler seem withdrawn? Is he less involved in family life?

◄ Is my child using an account that belongs to someone else?

Obviously, any of these scenarios can represent a part of the normal developmental process of a middle schooler. Some desire for privacy is normal. Staying up late can also be simply a matter of our child's changing circadian rhythms. And, as explained in previous chapters, at this age it's normal for our children to begin to break away from the family, to withdraw sometimes. That being said, we don't want to be in denial and automatically interpret such signs as "a stage" if our child may be in real danger.

TRUST YOUR INSTINCTS

One of the best resources at our disposal to keep our children safe is our parental instincts. Gavin de Becker, author of *Protecting the Gift: Keeping Children and Teenagers Safe (and Parents Sane)*, is widely recognized as our nation's foremost expert on the prediction and management of violence. He says that parents' instincts are always right with regard to our children's safety, for two reasons: our instincts are always based on something we've heard or seen that seems "off," and they always have our children's best interests at heart. The problem is that we often ignore our instincts. We may pass off our fears as unwarranted, because we don't want to be "overprotective." We may minimize them or even refuse to acknowledge them at all. De Becker emphasizes that "the human being is the only prey in nature that cooperates in its own victimization."

The bottom line in terms of protecting our kids is that we have to "trust our gut." If something doesn't feel right, it probably isn't.

THE COMMUNICATION COMPONENT

Of course, knowing the facts about safety on the Internet and trusting our instincts are only the first steps in keeping our middle schoolers safe. Maintaining open lines of communication with our middle schooler is the wisest method of protection we can employ, both to educate her about the dangers and to get information about her personal activities online.

The week following our discussion about Internet safety, Gary calls a family meeting to collect information from his children and share his concerns about the computer with them. After compliments and "old business," Gary says, "Kids, I want to talk about the computer." All three groan in varying degrees of distress.

"But, Dad," Martin protests, "I got off yesterday right when you told me to!"

Gary recognizes that this subject has started to place Martin, and perhaps all three of his children, on the defensive. Using "listening with heart," he acknowledges their reservations: "I bet you kids are worried that I'm going to lay down more rules. I'm not. I want to talk about computer facts."

"What do you mean, Daddy?" Cheryl asks.

"I'd like to know what you know about the computer and the Internet," Gary responds. "I'm willing to bet you know different things from what I know, and I want us to share our information."

> Use family meetings, not as a soapbox,
> but as an opportunity to share information and
> express concerns about the computer and your
> middle schooler's online activities.

Gary does an excellent job of seeking information here. Rather than blocking communication by jumping in and giving advice or acting as if he's the sole "keeper of the knowledge," he pulls the children into the discussion by encouraging a dialogue.

Jeremy looks suspicious. "Why?" he asks.

"For a couple of reasons," Gary answers. "One is that I'm interested in the games and activities you like online. And the other is that I want to make sure you are observing some protocol for keeping safe."

"What's protocol?" Cheryl wants to know.

"Well, there are certain facts about online safety that anyone who uses a computer needs to know," Gary explains. "Protocol means that there are guidelines we all need to follow, for a variety of reasons—so that our computer doesn't get a virus, for example, that wipes out the hard disk. But another, and very important, reason is that, unfortunately, there are sometimes strangers online who want to hurt kids."

At the same time that Martin cries, "Dad! We *know* all this," both Jeremy and Cheryl ask, "How could a stranger hurt someone on the computer?"

Martin takes this opportunity to say, "See? I knew we all had different types of information. Martin, would you explain to Jeremy and Cheryl what you know about strangers on the Internet?"

Gary does another excellent job in engaging Martin in the discussion by asking him to educate the younger children with whatever knowledge he has. Gary will have to be careful, however, that Martin doesn't feel as though Dad is "testing" him, with the intention of trapping or embarrassing him. If Martin were to respond defensively, Gary would want to reengage the technique of listening with heart to respond to Martin's feelings and reassure him that this is merely an opportunity for all of them to learn something.

Fortunately, Martin does not doubt Gary's motive, and he tells Jeremy and Cheryl what he knows about strangers online. As Martin speaks, Gary takes the opportunity to inject additional facts with comments such as "That's exactly right! And in addition . . . " In this way, Gary is able fill in the gaps in Martin's knowledge while making sure that all three children get a full explanation of the possible dangers.

When we communicate with our children about the dangers of sexual predation online, we mustn't present the facts in a way that forces them to make inferences. We should avoid euphemisms and generalities. For example, rather than stating, "There are people online who want to hurt others," we must be more explicit: "There are pedophiles online. These are adults who are sexually attracted to children and teens. They often pretend to be children themselves to gain a child's trust. They may ask the child or teen to meet them somewhere or may get enough information online to find out where the child lives or goes to school. They do this with the specific intention of abducting and physically or sexually hurting that child or teen."

You might now be thinking: "I can't say that! I can't tell my child that there are people out there who want to have sex with children! My child's too young to hear about this!" Or you might wonder, "But won't that information make my child fearful?"

Information keeps your middle schooler safe. Dispense it freely.

That line of reasoning is seriously flawed. The fact is that information is actually empowering. It allows our middle schoolers (and younger children like Cheryl) to evaluate their own safety, which doubles their level of protection.

As for our middle schoolers' being too young to hear about sex and specifically about sexual predation, I agree that it's heart wrenching to realize we can no longer keep our children safely cocooned away from the horrors of the world. To have to talk to them about violent sex before they even understand sex as an act of love goes against some of our most powerful instincts for protection. In fact, in trying to keep your children innocent, you may have been postponing the "sex talk" altogether.

I recognize that sex can be an intimidating topic to face, so we'll devote the entirety of Chapter 9 to the when, how, and why of talking to middle schoolers (and even younger children) about this sometimes tricky subject. For now, however, I think Gavin de Becker makes the strongest point about the necessity of discussing sex and sexual predation with our children when he quotes a police officer as saying, "Show me a child who knows nothing about sex and I'll show you a highly qualified victim."

If we do not teach our children the facts about Internet safety, online predators, and sex in plain, easy-to-understand language, we set them up to be potential victims.

INFORMATION WE NEED TO PRESENT

The guidelines that follow are based on recommendations from the FBI, PC Sentinal Software, the U.S. Department of Education, Gavin de Becker, and others. Be sure to share them with your middle schooler in addition to the foregoing information.

- ◄ Never communicate online with people you have not met off-line—even friends of friends. Predators can "infiltrate" a group of friends through its weakest link.
- ◄ Don't arrange a face-to-face meeting with anyone you meet online, even if the person appears to be your age and is someone you consider a friend. People can easily hide their true identities online, both because they can lie and because you can't hear their tone of voice or see their body language, which are two valuable indicators as to whether someone means us harm.
- ◄ Never upload pictures of yourself onto the Internet (including on social networking sites such as MySpace). Do not send pictures to an online service or to people you do not personally know. Even then, remember that by virtue of their being sent over the Web, they are essentially public property and can be forwarded to people you do not know. Make sure they are in good taste and cannot be misconstrued.

◄ Don't give out identifying information such as your name, home address, school name, or telephone number. Even seemingly innocuous information such as "I'm going to the Knicks game on Friday!" or "We have a big game with the Coyotes Thursday, and I'm playing first base!" can give predators information about where you live and what school you attend.

◄ Never download pictures or other files from an unknown source, as there is a good chance that sexually explicit images, language, or invitations are contained within (not to mention the possibility of a virus).

◄ Don't respond to messages or bulletin board postings that are suggestive, obscene, belligerent, or harassing. If you encounter any of this, tell a parent.

◄ Never use a credit card online without parental permission.

◄ Don't share your password with anyone, even with a friend.

◄ Never use bad language online or send mean messages. Remember that all information you send over the Internet is public and may be retrieved years or even decades later.

◄ Remember that whatever you are told online may or may not be true.

THE TWO MOST POWERFUL TOOLS

While the dangers of the Internet are real, and it's true that nothing is foolproof, we have two powerful tools at our disposal as parents of middle schoolers: relationship and communication. When we communicate information in the context of family meetings and engage our middle schooler in a respectful dialogue that allows us to find out what information she already has, we develop a cooperative method of protection. Thus, not only are we seeking to protect her, but also she is involved in protecting herself.

7

Encouraging Self-Esteem and Independence

When I was growing up, a lovely middle-aged couple lived next door to us: Robert and Camilla. Though childless, they were the quintessential aunt and uncle to all of the neighborhood kids.

The picture of domesticity, Camilla always had freshly baked cookies if we knocked on her door. Robert tended his yard—mowing, trimming, pruning the trees. He never hesitated to pluck a flower and hand it with a warm smile to anyone who walked by. Weekend after weekend, he'd haul out his ladder, climb to the top, and shape his trees with pruning shears, now and again pausing to put down the shears and run his hand lovingly through the leaves as if petting a favored animal.

His pruning, however, made Camilla nervous, and I'd often catch her, apron on and spatula in hand, calling up to him: "Robert! Be careful up there. Don't fall, now. Don't hurt yourself."

As the years passed, I noticed that although Robert still lovingly tended his yard and garden, now a truck would appear at regular intervals carrying a ladder and other lawn equipment. A man would hop out, set up the ladder, and prune Robert's trees. Rob watched from a distance, his face expressionless.

Years later, when I was grown and had children, Camilla passed away. I went to visit Rob, now a distinguished elderly gentleman with white hair. We sat in his living room with cups of tea, reminiscing about "the old days." Suddenly, I found myself curious. "Rob," I ventured, "I remember as a kid that you took such good care of your lawn." He smiled, and the corners of his eyes crinkled.

I continued, "I'm curious why you finally hired someone to come and do the trees for you. You seemed to take such pleasure in getting them just right."

The smile faded, and he leaned forward. "Julie," he said, "I'll tell you. When I was younger, I wouldn't have admitted this, but I'm old now, and Camilla's gone, and . . . well . . . " His voice trailed off.

When he spoke again, he was reflective and quiet: "I got afraid, sweetheart. I got afraid. It always made Camilla so nervous for me to be up there, I guess it just rubbed off. After a while, well, I just couldn't do it anymore. I'd take a look at the ladder, and my heart would start to beat faster. It just wasn't worth it . . . " His voice trailed off again, and then in a whisper he added, "But I do miss those trees."

I open this chapter with Rob's story because his love of trees, his love of his wife, and his loss of both break my heart. What happened to this grown man that he would give up something that he so clearly loved and in which he took so much pride? Was it a choice he made: wife or trees? Did Camilla give him an ultimatum? No. He stated it himself: he became afraid. Camilla's fear that something would happen to her beloved husband "just rubbed off." Robert, a middle-aged man, lost his courage.

WHAT IS COURAGE?

The word *courage* comes from the French word *coeur*, meaning "heart." It is intricately linked with our self-esteem, and it's the single biggest gift we can impart to our children, because the lessons they learn with the heart far outlast the lessons they learn with their minds.

> When we encourage our children,
> we speak directly to their hearts.

Our children begin life overflowing with courage. Just think for a moment about the courage it takes to learn to walk: to get up, fall down, get up, walk headlong into a table, fall down. Yet they never become afraid of walking. They keep at it. Their courage abounds.

So, what happens? Why does the self-esteem of these inherently courageous beings begin to falter?

THE COMPONENTS OF SELF-ESTEEM

There are many reasons that our children's self-esteem can fluctuate, because numerous components make up self-esteem. Chapter 1 presented a pyramid as a way to visualize those components, and in this chapter we revisit that metaphor. Our acceptance of our children and fulfilling their need to feel unconditionally loved, regardless of what they accomplish, forms the bottom level of the pyramid. It is

Garber, Garber, and Spizman's Self-Esteem Pyramid

Peer Influence
Parental Feedback
Real Accomplishments
Unconditional Positive Regard

the first, and most fundamental, way that we can build courage and self-esteem in our middle schooler.

The second level of the pyramid is "real accomplishments," which comprise the things that our children do that are measurable, things that they couldn't do before and can do now. Real accomplishments can be physical—the first time your middle schooler makes a home run, for example. They can also be academic, such as when your seventh-grader struggles with a difficult math problem and gets it right. For Jordan and Kevin, our "overwhelmed slackers" from Chapter 2, the struggle to get organized and manage their homework became "real accomplishments" when they conquered these tasks, and their self-esteem grew in the process.

For our middle schoolers in general, each step in their burgeoning independence represents an opportunity for us to support the development of their self-esteem.

The Importance of Struggle

In order for real accomplishments to work toward the development of self-esteem, they must be accompanied by a small amount of struggle. Children for whom certain things come easily may not have high self-esteem. You might wonder why this would be the case. Perhaps the best way to illustrate the concept is with a story:

A teacher sends his student into the woods to watch a butterfly emerging from a cocoon. The student watches and waits, and the butterfly struggles to free itself from the cocoon. The student begins to worry about the poor butterfly. He watches some more and waits, and finally, his heart is filled with compassion for the poor butterfly's struggle. Very gently, he reaches over and helps the butterfly out of its cocoon. The butterfly flies for a few feet and then falls to the ground and dies. The student begins to cry and runs back to his teacher. "Why," he demands, "why did the butterfly die?" The teacher replies, "When you reached in and helped the butterfly out of its cocoon, you deprived it of the opportunity to strengthen its wings in the struggle."

When our children struggle with the tasks they're given in life, both the ordinary and the extraordinary, they are strengthening their wings. Struggle is an essential component in building self-esteem.

The caveat is that, in order for struggle to work in this way, there must be neither too much nor too little. Consider the following analogy: If your child is in a boat, and the boat is coursing down the river, but your child is not paddling at all, she's not going to feel a sense of accomplishment, because the river is doing the work, and not she. This is what good grades are for some children: they don't count as a real accomplishment, because the child hasn't had to work at them. In addition, because the child is not accustomed to struggling, the minute something occurs that requires her to struggle, she's likely to give up, believing it to be too hard. Thus, the possibility of that next task's becoming a "real accomplishment" is also lost.

> **Struggle raises self-esteem, but it must be neither too much struggle nor too little.**

On the other hand, a different child may be paddling as hard as he can, but if the boat is not moving forward, he's not going to feel a sense of accomplishment either. In fact, struggling that hard and not getting anywhere is likely to cause him to give up too. That's part of what happened to Jordan in Chapter 2. He might have started out paddling, but because his boat wasn't moving, the struggle to keep up with his homework became too burdensome, so he just let it drop.

Praise Doesn't Help

Some parents might wonder if they can help their child develop self-esteem in either of the situations just described by commenting on how well the child is doing. For example, if you have a naturally gifted student who has low self-esteem, why doesn't it work to tell her how terrific it is that she's getting straight As? Or, if your child is trying hard but not getting anywhere, why doesn't your assurance that he's doing a great job mean something?

The truth is that praise does nothing to bolster self-esteem, yet it's a common mistake for parents to think that if they heap on enough praise, their children will feel good about themselves.

Returning to the boat analogy, imagine standing on the bank of the river, praising each of the children in the scenarios. You're shouting: "I'm so proud of you! Look what you've accomplished! You're doing a great job!" The child who's not paddling at all is thinking: "I'm not accomplishing anything; I'm not even paddling. It's the river that's making the progress." The child who's paddling as hard as he can but not seeing progress is thinking: "I'm not doing anything; my boat isn't getting anywhere. I have to paddle as hard as I can just to stay in the same place." Praise doesn't affect our children's self-esteem, because true self-esteem comes from an internal assessment, not an external one.

Boosting Self-Esteem Through Encouragement

So, if praise doesn't help, what does? How can we support the development of our children's self-esteem and build their courage if not by praising them? The answer lies in using encouragement instead. Encouragement, which literally means "to instill with courage," is different from praise in that it focuses on the effort that our child makes, while praise focuses on the results of that effort.

But what does it mean to focus on effort rather than result? Perhaps the best way to see the difference is by comparing the two side by side:

What we don't want to do	What we *do* want to do
Focus on results:	Focus on effort:
"You got an A! I'm so proud of you!"	"You worked hard in science this year."
"You made a home run!"	"You've been practicing your swing, I see!"
"I'm so proud of you for getting the lead in the school play!"	"I really enjoyed hearing you work on your monologue for the audition."

It can be problematic not to include praise of the results when we focus on effort. For example, it's difficult not to say, "You worked hard in science this year, and look, it really paid off, because you got an A!" However, if we instead allow our preteen to make the inference that his hard work paid off, he can begin to recognize his "real accomplishments." For example, limiting your remark to "You worked hard in science this year" allows your middle schooler to finish the sentence in his head: "*and* I got an A for my efforts!"

What happens, though, when a child isn't working hard—or, even more challenging, when a child won't even make an effort? Stephanie faced just such a problem with her daughter. Aimee is a student for whom straight-A report cards come naturally. Despite this record, her self-esteem is extremely low. In addition, activities in which she might have an opportunity to struggle and experience a "real accomplishment" are often things she's hesitant to try.

Stephanie explains: "I'm at a loss as to how I can help Aimee. I mean, I can focus on effort by saying, 'I see you're working hard in school' and let her infer that the good grades stem from that, but she's not really working that hard, so it would kind of be a lie. And the things that would be a struggle for her—I mean, she won't even walk to school by herself—are things she doesn't even try to do, so I can't focus on her effort there either."

DEVELOPMENTAL READINESS

When our middle schooler is hesitant about making an effort, either because she's afraid or because she has simply decided the effort isn't worth it, we have an opportunity to stimulate her courage so that she can experience a "real accomplishment."

Let's put Aimee's hesitancy about walking to school by herself to the test. The first thing that Stephanie needs to determine is whether this is a reasonable expectation. In other words, is Aimee developmentally ready to try this? One way to determine if your expectations for your child are developmentally reasonable is to ask yourself, "What are my child's friends doing that he is not doing?"

This question is one way of measuring a child's abilities against the developmental norm. While there are certainly textbooks that go to great lengths to describe what's normal and appropriate for children at different ages, they often don't take into account the environment or society within which the child is being raised. For example, it might be developmentally appropriate for a first-grader from a small town in Texas to walk a few blocks to school by himself, while this freedom is often not appropriate for a New York City child until he reaches middle school.

Built-In Measuring Sticks

There's no question that, in general, it's not a good idea to compare our son or daughter with other children lest we lose our sense of our child as a unique individual. Nevertheless, it is apparent that our children are doing exactly that: measuring themselves against their peers. We aren't raising our children in isolation, and they are completely aware of what their peers feel comfortable doing. If your child sees that his peers are capable of something that he doesn't feel comfortable doing, he might begin to feel that he's lacking in some way, that there's something wrong with him.

Thus, it's helpful to use the activities of other middle schoolers as a measuring stick. This gauge can give us an indication of the areas in which our child needs support in order to build his self-esteem.

Now, all of this is not to say that if your child's peers are all going to see R-rated movies, you should allow your child to do so as well. Bending your values will *not* increase your middle schooler's self-esteem. Rather, you need to concentrate on tasks that feature skills and abilities, such as walking to school, making his own breakfast or lunch, or doing her own laundry, to name a few.

> *Don't* change your values. *Do* look
> at skills and abilities.

Taking a Child's Individuality into Consideration

While we can sometimes use our children's peers as a general yardstick for the developmental tasks that are normal at certain ages, we must always remember that each of our children is a unique individual and should be respected as such. For example, if all of your child's friends know how to ride a bicycle, but your child just doesn't care to learn, it's not something that you should force him to do. Some things are simply individual preferences, and not everyone has to be able to do everything in order to be a well-rounded individual. This is also important to keep in mind if you know your child has any developmental disorders. Each circumstance should be evaluated individually against the backdrop of who your child is.

Are Your Expectations Appropriate?

Look for:
◄ Developmental readiness
◄ Individual capability

Ask yourself:
◄ Is this an optional skill or a
necessary one?

For Stephanie's daughter, Aimee, walking to school is not an optional skill, like riding a bike. Because eventually Aimee will need to know how to get places on her own, this is a necessary skill related to overall independence. She lives only a few blocks from her school, in a safe community, and at age twelve, she's as tall as her mother, so she can't be targeted as a victim because of size. Her neighborhood friends have been walking since sixth grade. In fact, they often invite Aimee to come along with them, but Aimee refuses. Walking to school is a normal activity that others in her age-group do without fear, and it's one she could be doing as well.

CALLING FORTH INDEPENDENCE

Now that Stephanie has determined that walking to school is an appropriate expectation for her to have of Aimee, she can tap the skill of "calling forth independence" to stimulate her daughter's courage. This involves two components:

◄ Presenting the expectation in a clear, firm, and respectful way
◄ Leaving enough time for your child to process the information and work out a plan of action

For example, Stephanie might say, "Aimee, next Wednesday I'd like you to get yourself to school." This statement gives Aimee several days to have an emotional reaction, to process the information, and to get support in working out a plan.

Once Stephanie has done this, she'll want to draw from a variety of tools that she's already learned to encourage Aimee. "Listening with heart," "cooperative communication," and "acknowledging ability" are some that might be useful.

Let's see what happens when Stephanie goes home with this new information and returns two weeks later.

Aimee's "Real Accomplishment"

Stephanie arrives at our group with a spring in her step, excited to tell us how "calling forth independence" went with Aimee:

Stephanie is in the kitchen, cleaning up after dinner, when Aimee comes downstairs after doing her homework. "I'm fiiiiiiiinnnnnally finished," Aimee says as she drops into a chair.

Steph wipes her hands on a dish towel, rounds the counter, and gives her daughter a hug. "That's wonderful!" she says. "Listen, I wanted to tell you something about next Thursday. I have a few errands that I need to run, and I want to be sure to finish by noon, so I'm going to need you to get yourself to school that day."

Aimee's eyes widen. "*What?* Mom! That's not fair!"

"Tell me why it doesn't seem fair to you," Stephanie says in a sympathetic voice, sitting down in the chair next to Aimee's.

"It's just not! You always take me to school. I . . . I have all these books to carry. My backpack is too heavy, and I might even have to turn in my science fair project that day. I can't walk with all that."

Aimee is clearly nervous about the expectation that Stephanie has stated and is looking for as many "reasonable" excuses as possible to convince her mother that she "needs" to be taken to school. It would be easy for Mom to take the bait here and get caught up in reasoning with her daughter about "the facts": how they could clean out her backpack so it wouldn't be too heavy, how Aimee could leave textbooks she doesn't need at school, and so on. To stay on track, Stephanie will be better off if she sticks with feelings.

Don't get caught up in the facts. Do focus on feelings.

Stephanie continues by "listening with heart": "It sounds as if you're uncomfortable about this plan. It's normal to be a little nervous the first time you try something new."

"It's not that!" Aimee exclaims. "I really have too many books and stuff. You have to take me to school!"

"I understand that you'd like me to," Stephanie tells her, "and I can't that day." (Stephanie does a commendable job of setting a firm boundary here.) "What can you think of to help make this more manageable for you?"

"Nothing!" Aimee bursts into tears and runs out of the room.

We can see that as Stephanie moves from "listening with heart" to "cooperative communication," Aimee begins to struggle. Mom's firm boundary ("I can't that day") has begun the process that will lead to a "real accomplishment" for her daughter. If Stephanie were to waver here—if she were to "take back the boundary" and say, "OK, it's all right; I'll drive you."—she would be doing the equivalent of what the boy in the butterfly story does: helping the butterfly out of its cocoon.

Don't "help the butterfly out of its cocoon!"

Two days pass before the subject arises again. This can feel like a long time for some parents. Living without a resolution to an upcoming situation is difficult, but it is often necessary. Stephanie has wisely chosen to let the subject drop to give Aimee enough time to process the information.

Aimee approaches Stephanie as she's putting her makeup on. "Mom?"

Stephanie smiles as she glances up at Aimee's reflection in the bathroom mirror. "Yes?"

"I found out yesterday that my science fair project is due on Thursday, so you do have to take me to school that day."

"Ah," Stephanie says, remaining calm. "Well, how do you want to handle that?"

"What do you mean?" Aimee asks. "I need you to take me to school that day."

"I hear that you have to get your science fair project to school, and you know that's the day you have to walk. So, what can we do to figure this out?"

"I *hate* you!" Aimee bursts into tears again and makes her usual dash for the exit.

It would have been so tempting for Stephanie to acquiesce at this point and agree to take Aimee to school. In fact, many parents might wonder: "What's the big deal? Why not just make her walk to school another day?" The answer is that there will be many times that it seems "reasonable" to help our butterfly out of her cocoon, but the effect will be the same: if she doesn't struggle, she won't be strengthening her wings.

Now, I don't mean to imply that you should be rigid. In fact, rigidity is often the downfall of effective parenting. Still, it's OK to require our children to figure out solutions to normal, safe, yet challenging situations. Think ahead to when your child is in high school or college, or has a job. She will have to come up with solutions to problems similar to getting an unwieldy science fair project to school without you there. By requesting that Aimee do it this time, Stephanie is using this opportunity to teach Aimee to draw on other resources besides her mother.

**Our middle schooler needs to learn to
draw on resources other than a parent.**

After school that day, Stephanie approaches Aimee and initiates a conversation by "listening with heart":

"Hey, Aimee. You were pretty mad at me this morning." Aimee glares at her mother but says nothing. "Looks as if you're still pretty angry. Do you want to talk about it?"

"No!" Aimee turns away.

"I guess you're feeling a little overwhelmed with having to get yourself to school on Thursday, huh?"

"It's just not fair, Mom!" Aimee wails. "You always take me to school. I don't want to have to go by myself."

"I know, sweetheart. It's hard. I know you're disappointed that I can't help you out that day. I'm wondering if you can think of someone who could?"

"Like who?" Aimee's eyes well up with tears. "My friends walk to school; no one drives."

"Well, what do you think would happen if you walked with them and asked one of them to help you carry some of your things?"

"They have enough to carry, Mom!" Aimee's voice trembles. "Please, I need you to take me to school."

"I know, hon. It sounds as if your science fair project is pretty cumbersome. I'm wondering what would happen if we took it over to the school on Wednesday? That might make it easier to walk to school on Thursday."

"Mom, they probably won't let me do that. Why can't you just take me?"

Aimee is persistent, that's for sure. And most middle schoolers will be. It's part of the struggle.

"Aimee," Stephanie says as she sits beside her and takes her hand, "this is something you can do. I know it's awkward and uncomfortable. I also know that you will come up with a solution. I'm here to help you figure it out if you need me." Stephanie gives Aimee's hand a quick squeeze and then stands and walks away.

Let's pause here to note a few highlights about this conversation:

◄ Even though Aimee turns away at the beginning, Stephanie continues in an empathetic mode, which opens Aimee back up to engaging in the discussion. While this won't always happen, it's worth making a few empathetic comments to a noncommunicative middle schooler to see if you can reengage her.

◄ Stephanie valiantly stays on track and does not respond directly to Aimee's requests for her to change her mind about driving. Rather, she moves smoothly to the next step in cooperative communication: brainstorming. ("I know, hon. . . . I'm wondering what would happen if . . . ")

◄ Stephanie is careful not to connect her sentences with the word *but*. Remember that "but" negates what comes before it. If Stephanie had said, "I know your science fair project is pretty unwieldy, *but* I'm not going to drive you," she would have negated the respect she was showing for Aimee's perspective.

◄ Finally, Mom ends the conversation by "acknowledging ability," saying, "This is something you can do," and she offers her support ("I'm here to help . . . ") without changing her boundary.

The Anticlimax

I know you're wondering how this all ends. I've packed this story with so much detail to illustrate the length of time that "calling forth independence" can take, as well as the variety of techniques you may have to use in the process. In addition, middle schoolers can be both persistent and persuasive, and it's incumbent on you to remain firm about the boundaries you set when you're encouraging real accomplishments.

For Stephanie and Aimee, the conclusion to their story is so anti-climactic that it's almost laughable:

It's around 10:00 P.M. when Stephanie arrives at Aimee's bedroom door to say good night. Aimee is reading. Stephanie walks to her and kisses her on the forehead, reciting their nighttime ritual: "I love you; sleep tight; don't let the bedbugs bite." Aimee smiles, and as Stephanie is leaving, Aimee says: "Oh, Mom? Just so you know, I called Mary, and she's going to help me get my project to school on Thursday. She has a cart-thing that she'll bring over, and we'll go together." Stephanie nods and, in a matter-of-fact way that belies the struggle they've just undergone, says, "Sounds good. See you in the morning."

Just as the butterfly's flight after emerging from the cocoon is seemingly effortless, so too our children's real accomplishment at the end of a struggle may appear to have needed no effort whatsoever. This is the way it should be: it's the struggle that's important after all.

WHAT HAPPENS WHEN THE FEAR IS REASONABLE?

Olivia speaks up: "I have something to tell the group. You know Jordan is going to that new middle school?" Heads nod. "Well, there's this bully in his class—he's really big, and he's been threatening Jordan that he's going to beat him up after school. So, Jordan's just been ignoring him, but last week, this guy was waiting for him on the path coming home, and he picked a fight. Jordan came home with a black eye, and now he's afraid to walk home by himself."

Olivia eyes brim with tears as she continues. "We told the school, and the boy was expelled. But Jordan is still afraid. And truthfully," she adds shakily, "I don't blame him."

No words can describe how furious this type of incident makes me. In my years as a parent educator, I've seen tragedy strike countless times: children who are bullied or beaten up like Jordan, others who lose a parent or a sibling, several who developed or combated a life-threatening disease. But no matter how often I've encountered life's unjustness, it never, ever gets easier. Each time, I, along with the parents I counsel, just want to scream at the world: "Leave our children alone. Let them grow without disaster, without adversity. There's time enough later. Just leave them alone!"

Obviously, and unfortunately, none of us can prevent life from happening to our children. What we must do, then, is support our children when the unthinkable happens and give them the necessary tools to handle the inevitabilities in their lives.

"The thing is," Olivia sniffles, "he was so independent. And you know he's not that good a student, so his independence was one way I could see that he felt competent—because he could get himself around town. And now that's gone. He's shaky. And he doesn't want to go out. I've been taking him to school and picking him up for the past week, and he needs me to reassure him that I'll be standing right there when he comes out of the building. Do I, should I, keep taking him to school, or do I need to make him do it himself?"

When something scary happens to our children, it's normal and appropriate for them to feel shaky, to lose courage. In fact, I would be puzzled if Jordan weren't nervous about going to school and coming home by himself so soon after being beaten up. Nevertheless, there will come a time when we have to encourage our child to try again, lest the child remain disheartened forever.

"Getting Back on the Horse"

One of the hardest things parents have to do is help our children "get back up on the horse" when something bad happens to them. While extra protection, support, and nurturing are appropriate for a while, as the intensity of the experience begins to fade, we have to marshal our own resources and encourage our children to go back out into the world.

This is hard for many reasons, not the least of which is that we're scared too. We think to ourselves: "What if we send them back out into the world and something happens again? How could we live with ourselves knowing that we encouraged them to do something that proved to be unsafe?"

I wish we could wrap our children in cotton padding and protect them from the world. And one of the primary jobs of parents *is* to protect them. But we also have the duty to prepare them. Children who have been overprotected come to believe that the entire world isn't safe. I've seen perpetually unhappy adults frozen with indecision about the smallest matters: whether to order coffee or tea, to walk somewhere or drive, to call a friend or not. These adults lead tortured lives, thinking that any decision they make will be catastrophic. They are people who don't and will never function normally in the world, because somewhere along the line they got the message, "The world isn't safe, and you aren't competent to handle it." Our children need to learn to live in a world where there is uncertainty and where they will experience both the good and the bad.

> Our children have to learn to
> live in a world that includes both the
> good and the bad.

Now, I'm not saying we should deliberately send our children out into an unsafe situation: "Go play in the traffic, honey!" I am saying that it's our job to make sure they lead normal, independent lives, which means they have to develop resources for coping with the situations, and even dangers, that exist in their environment.

Taking It Slowly

So, the question begs to be asked: When? When do we send our children back out into the world after something happens to them? How, exactly, does the timing work?

Obviously, the answer will depend in part on what your child has been through. Clearly, we need to give each child time to heal after a crisis—especially psychologically. For some children, healing may take a few weeks. For others, it could take much longer.

In Jordan's case, Olivia should give him a couple of weeks to see how he's doing before encouraging him to walk home by himself again. She will want to wait until she sees the majority of the fear fade. Maybe she'll notice that he's stopped asking for reassurance that she'll be there after school, even when he still expects her to be. For Olivia, and for you, my best advice is to trust yourself to know when your child is ready. That being said, if a child is still exhibiting extreme withdrawal or fear after a couple of months, you might need to get outside help for him to work through this.

Therapy Can Help

Parents should be open to the idea that in some cases, short-term therapy can be helpful when our children have had a traumatic experience. The very nature of our relationship as parents with our children precludes our being able to serve in the therapist's role. When a child has been exposed to violence, serious illness, or death, the family can sometimes use a helping hand. It relieves the parents of some of the burden, and an outside "voice" is often heard differently by a child from the way he hears his mother or father.

Preparing to Handle It Yourself

As traumatic as getting beaten up by a school bully is, it's unlikely that Jordan will need therapy, and Olivia wants to be prepared to handle the situation herself. She asks: "Let's say that in a couple of weeks, I see that he's not as scared. Then what do I do?"

"Just what Stephanie did," I explain, "only break it into even smaller pieces, and be up-front about getting him back on his feet."

When a child has undergone a traumatic experience, it's unwise to pretend that nothing happened. The more up-front we can be, the better. Thus, Olivia could say something like this: "I know you've been nervous about going back and forth to school by yourself after you were mugged, and I don't blame you. Now we have to figure out a way to get you back on your feet so you can feel comfortable again."

Creating a Step-by-Step Plan

Olivia gave Jordan a couple of weeks and then introduced the subject of traveling by himself in the way we described. Using "cooperative communication" and a lot of "listening with heart," she supported him in coming up with a step-by-step plan. Together, they decided that the first week, she would walk him close enough to the school where she could watch him enter the building safely. The same plan was enacted for after school: she met him across the street from the building, rather than right outside the door. After a week, she encouraged him to walk a few blocks by himself both ways, meeting him on a corner.

The next step called for Jordan to travel to school by himself in the morning, with Olivia still meeting him for the walk home, albeit several blocks away. In addition, they discussed strategies that Jordan could use if he felt he was being approached in an unsafe manner again, including what he could do and to which safe locations he could run. Within about a month, Jordan became comfortable traveling on his own again.

Handling Your Own Feelings

Olivia was able to trust herself to know when Jordan could be encouraged to be independent again, but this transition doesn't always feel possible. After something like this happens, we can get so frightened that we just want to pack up and move to a deserted island somewhere so that our children would be safe.

Parents may also need therapy after a child's traumatic event, because it can be hard to overcome our own fears independently. Other times, going through the same step-by-step process that you've asked your child to employ can do the trick, because each step gives you the experience of increased safety. You can also overcome your fear sometimes by changing your "think-feel-do cycle."

We talked at length about the think-feel-do cycle in Chapter 2. Becoming aware of our thoughts gives us an opportunity to change them, which, in turn, will change our feelings. If Olivia were having difficulty breaking out of a negative cycle of fear after Jordan's incident, she might sit down and analyze the thoughts that are triggering her anxiety. They might be: "He'll get hurt again." "Next time, it will be worse." "The world isn't safe."

Once aware of these thoughts, she can deliberately try to change them. She might choose: "The world is relatively safe." "He's going to be fine." "The school expelled the boy, and the danger is past." This type of deliberate "self-talk," used almost like a mantra, can radically alter the cycles in which we find ourselves.

Sometimes, though, and with good reason, parents have difficulty changing their thoughts. After all, when something like this happens, you might wonder: "How can I say to myself, 'He's going to be fine,' when he *wasn't* fine? How do I *know* that my child will be safe?"

First of all, note that changing the think-feel-do cycle is just one of many techniques for confronting life's uncertainties. You might not be able to change your thoughts with that particular technique, and you might need the experiential approach (walking your child step-by-step through the situations that feel unsafe), or you might need a therapeutic approach. You have to ascertain what's right for you.

As for how we can *know* that our child will be safe, the ultimate answer is that we can't. As a parent, you just don't know. But sometimes it's helpful to weigh the difference between possibility and probability to determine whether we should encourage a real accomplishment for our child.

Possible Versus Probable

The *American Heritage Dictionary* defines *possible* as "of uncertain likelihood," while it defines *probable* as "likely to happen or to be true." When we're fearful, it can pay to ask ourselves, "Is it possible for something bad *to* happen, or is it probable that something bad *will* happen?

Let's go back for a moment to my dear neighbors from childhood, Robert and Camilla. Was it possible for Robert to hurt himself when pruning the trees? Sure. It's *possible* that he would cut himself with the pruning shears. It's *possible* that he would fall off the ladder. It's *possible* that he would accidentally jostle a wasp's nest and be stung and have an allergic reaction and wind up in the hospital and have to go on disability and . . . well, you get the picture. Anything is *possible*. The real question is: Was it *probable* that he would cut himself? No. That he would fall off the ladder? No. That he would accidentally brush up against a wasp's next? No.

So, given that it wasn't a probability, was it worth his "assured safety" for him to give up doing something that he clearly loved so much? Absolutely not.

Obviously, when the subject is our child rather than an adult, and when something that was only a possibility actually comes to pass—like Jordan's being bullied and beaten up—it's a bit trickier because it's more emotionally laden. Clearly, if we think that something will probably happen again, we want to take appropriate cautionary measures. However, the fact that something has happened once does not necessarily mean that it will repeat itself. Moreover, even when something is probable, we shouldn't assume that it will actually happen.

> **"A thousand probabilities do not make one fact."—Italian proverb**

In the end, we have to weigh the possibility or probability against the cost. Given that Jordan's school is in a relatively safe neighborhood, that he traveled to and from school safely for months, and that the bully was expelled, Olivia decided that empowering Jordan to "get back on the horse" was in his best interests.

Each of our middle schoolers, in these years and beyond, will face ordinary and extraordinary circumstances that will challenge them. The challenges may be physical, emotional, or academic. They may be simple or complex. They may even evoke fear. Yet when we encourage our children to face these challenges head-on, **we are helping them to strengthen their wings. And I can promise you this: your child will fly higher and faster and farther *if* you don't shy away from the struggle.**

8

The Push for Independence

"What should we do if we want to lower our child's self-esteem?" Stephanie asks.

I look at her quizzically. "Lower a child's self-esteem? Why would you want to do that?"

"Well, I told you that I think Aimee has too little self-esteem, but my eleven-year-old, Daniel, is the exact opposite! I think he has too much self-esteem. He's always bragging about all the things he can do, but he can't really do them. For example, he'll tell you he knows how to ride a horse. He doesn't know how to ride a horse! He's ridden a horse only once. He didn't fall off, but he's not an experienced rider. He could put himself in danger by saying he knows how to do things he doesn't really know how to do. It's not safe, right? Don't you think he has too much self-esteem?"

SELF-ESTEEM VERSUS HUBRIS

There's really no such thing as having too much self-esteem. When children brag that they can do things they really can't do, it's more likely to be a bit of hubris, which is different from self-esteem.

Hubris refers to an arrogance, an unjustified overconfidence that's not based in real accomplishments. Self-esteem is internal and refers to a child's sense of confidence and competence in the world. Hubris is external or behavioral, usually taking the form of bragging or bravado, and may be used by a middle schooler to cover up shaky or low self-esteem. True self-esteem shows itself in a child's willingness to take a known risk for a known purpose.

Almost all middle school children will exhibit a bit of hubris from time to time. Like Daniel, they may brag about being able to do things of which they're not really capable and may even actually believe that they can do these things. But it would be a mistake to conclude that they need their self-esteem taken down a notch when, to the contrary, every child needs all the self-esteem that can be had to meet life's challenges.

This doesn't mean that you should be alarmed if your child exhibits hubris, at least some of the time. As many parents can attest, because our preteen's sense of self is still forming, he may waffle between hubris, confidence, and low self-esteem weekly (or even daily!).

The obligation of parents is neither to beat down nor to prop up our children's self-esteem. Rather, we need to support its healthy development by giving our children a base of unconditional love and the opportunity to experience real accomplishments in the real world. In addition, we need to avoid overprotecting them.

PROTECTION VERSUS OVERPROTECTION

As I mentioned in Chapter 7, it's our responsibility both to protect our children and to prepare them to live in the real world. Therefore, when your son brags about things he can do, when your daughter gets your heart racing because you're worried that she'll put herself in a risky situation, you must evaluate whether your actions or words are protective or *over*protective. Squashing children's self-esteem will not keep them safe; protecting them will. This brings us to the difference between protection and overprotection. Let's look at the various forms of overprotection or "self-esteem squashing" in which we can engage. Then we'll see how Stephanie can protect her son without diminishing his confidence.

Overprotection of our middle schoolers can take any of the following forms:

- ◄ Restricting their independence unnecessarily
- ◄ Resolving conflicts for them
- ◄ Bailing them out of tough situations
- ◄ Doing things for them that they could do for themselves

Let's explore some concrete examples of each of these items.

Restricting Independence Unnecessarily

We unnecessarily restrict our middle schooler's independence when a particular situation is low risk and yet we still won't allow our middle schooler to participate. We discussed an example of this in Chapter 7, regarding preteens traveling independently. Other examples might be having no Internet access because you're fearful of online predators, forbidding your child to swim in the ocean because you're afraid of sharks, or not allowing your child to climb a tree because of the danger of falling. We often restrict independence when we see outcomes that are "possible" as being "probable" and allow fear rather than reason to dictate our decisions. As our children develop, it's wise to evaluate and reevaluate actual risk versus imaginary risk and then allow appropriate independence accordingly.

Resolving Conflicts for the Child

Conflict between our middle schooler and the other people in his life is inevitable. A teacher may give him a lower grade than he thinks he deserves; a friend may fail to invite him to a birthday party; he may complain about the treatment he's receiving from a sibling. Conflict is a normal part of life, and we rob our children of the opportunity to learn how to handle difficult situations when we overprotect them by providing solutions rather than letting them work it out. Each time we "fix" a conflict for them, they lose confidence in their capabilities. Lowered confidence means lower self-esteem. In Chapter 10, we'll discuss how to support conflict resolution in a way that builds self-esteem—especially as it applies to the sibling relationship.

Bailing the Child Out of Tough Situations

As with conflict, situations are bound to arise for our middle schooler that are challenging in some way. She may forget to write a paper until the day before it's due; he may mismanage his allowance and find he's run out of money before the end of the week; she may forget to bring home a book that she needs that evening for homework. Many parents have the tendency to jump into action when these things happen: they sit up until 2:00 A.M. feeding information to their preteen so the paper gets done; they give her a loan on next week's allowance to tide her over; they run to school to pick up the book she forgot.

Bailing out our middle schoolers does them a great disservice, in terms of both self-esteem and personal growth. Remember that when our children struggle, it "strengthens their wings." Allowing your child to come up with solutions in tough situations builds her internal resources. She must learn to cope with life's many adversities and with the mistakes she will inevitably make along the way. Letting her experience the consequences of her mistakes and supporting her in problem solving, rather than bailing her out, will increase her self-esteem and make her more resourceful.

Doing Things for the Child That the Child Could Do Independently

A case in point of this last aspect of overprotection is Stephanie and Aimee's situation, from Chapter 7. Stephanie consistently took Aimee to school, even though Aimee was capable of going without her. Other examples might be preparing your middle schooler's lunch on a daily basis, or running to get him a soda from the fridge because he's "in the middle of something." As simple as these examples may appear, they can add up to a significant loss of self-esteem. Of course, there are larger examples as well: there are parents who do their middle schooler's homework for them, who micromanage getting the homework into the backpack every night—putting it there themselves if they find their preteen failed to do so, and so on. When we do things, small or large, for our middle schooler that he could do for himself, we are robbing him of independence and ultimately of self-esteem.

COMMUNICATING WITHOUT DISCOURAGING

"But, Julie," Stephanie interjects, "doesn't Daniel's hubris about horseback riding fall into the category of protection, rather than overprotection? He doesn't know how to ride, and he's going to camp this summer. He's going to tell them that he's an experienced rider. What if they put him in a level that's too advanced for him, and he gets hurt? Shouldn't I discourage him and remind him that he doesn't know how to ride?"

If the truth be told, I really admire Daniel's self-assurance! Just think about it: at what other point in his life will he feel so expansive? So ready to throw his arms around life, to try things with such bravado? At some point, all of us come face-to-face with reality and learn that we are ultimately a measure of our limitations—of what we actually *can* do—not of what we *think* we can do. But why have Daniel learn that lesson at such a young age?

Now, I'm not disagreeing with Stephanie altogether. There's no debate that, as parents, we are duty bound to keep our children safe.

But remember, we don't achieve our children's safety by robbing them of self-esteem.

> Relationship has to remain
> at the heart of every interaction we have
> with our middle schooler.

For example, consider the effect on Daniel if Stephanie were to say: "Daniel, you're not a good horseback rider. You have virtually no experience. Don't go into the camp telling them that you know how to ride when you don't. It's not safe." One of two things likely will happen. Either it will "shake the chrysalis," causing him to feel resentful and creating distance in their relationship, or he'll start second-guessing himself about all of the areas in which he feels confident, and that may lead to a fear of failure.

Keeping Relationship at the Heart

When our middle schooler's level of confidence looks as though it might put him in a dangerous situation, the very first thing we have to consider is *how* to communicate our concern. Rather than letting loose with any words that come to mind, we should pause and reflect on the following question: Is how I'm about to communicate going to *build* my relationship with my middle schooler?

If it's not going to build the relationship, two courses of action are available to you:

- ◄ Option one. Say nothing—or, in the words of one of my group members, "Zippy the lippy."
- ◄ Option two. Use a technique that will allow you to communicate in an encouraging way rather than a discouraging way.

In Stephanie's predicament, she could "zippy the lippy" with Daniel but call the camp and relay her concern to the administrators instead. This would remove the problem from her relationship with Daniel and place the responsibility appropriately in the hands of the camp director and counselors who will actually be monitoring his safety while he's there.

Stephanie tried calling the camp but ended up leaving a message. Having then to wait for a callback was making her increasingly anxious, so she decided to see if she could use some of the techniques we've been discussing to address Daniel directly about her concerns without diminishing his self-esteem.

Stephanie Follows Up

Honoring the quality of reciprocity, Stephanie begins by determining both her own and Daniel's specific needs. She needs to be reassured that Daniel's exuberant attitude about his horseback-riding ability won't put him in danger, while Daniel needs to explore the feeling of independence and freedom that horseback riding can provide without worrying that he's "not good enough."

Once she's identified each of their needs, she scripts herself and then uses the "sandwich" technique to communicate. She says: "Daniel, I'm so excited about your going to camp this year! One thing I love is that it gives you an opportunity to try new things and improve on the skills that you're learning. I also know you need to be out from under my 'overprotective eye' and have a little more independence."

Daniel rolls his eyes, but Stephanie forges on: "I guess I need a little reassurance from you, though, because I'm feeling concerned that the camp might put you in a level of horseback riding that's too high, which could be dangerous. I know it's probably silly to worry; it's just that I love you so much. I know you have a good head on your shoulders, though, and you won't overstretch and do something you aren't actually capable of."

"Oh, Mom," Daniel says, shaking his head in disgust. "You always worry about everything; I'll be fine," he says dismissively and turns his attention back to the computer.

While at first, this overture seems not to have accomplished much, Stephanie may actually have achieved more than she might think. Let's look at how skillfully she's handled this exchange before we issue a progress report.

Note that for the first layer of "bread" in the sandwich, Stephanie uses a positive statement to set the tone of the communication. She then acknowledges Daniel's need for independence.

In the "meat" of her sandwich, Stephanie mentions her own need (reassurance of his safety) and uses an "I statement" to express her concern: "I'm feeling concerned . . . "

In the final layer of the sandwich, she expresses her love and uses "exhibiting trust" as a way to plant the seed that might help Daniel focus on balancing his confidence with his actual skills.

THE VALUE OF PLANTING SEEDS

"Planting seeds" in our middle schooler is similar to planting seeds in a garden. We carefully deposit the seed. We cover it gently. We water it faithfully. Then, we wait.

Our middle schoolers are rich, fertile soil, ready to soak up the sun and water and willing to support the growth of the seeds we plant. However, a good gardener is patient. He doesn't water the seed, wait five minutes, and, when nothing happens, complain, "This is useless!" He doesn't dig up the seed before it's had a chance to gestate. And once the green shoot has finally forced its way through the earth, he doesn't yank on it to get it to grow faster.

Parents of middle schoolers have to be master gardeners. Patience, faith, and appropriate support will help ensure that our plantings eventually blossom and bear fruit.

Despite Daniel's apparent dismissal of Stephanie's concern, she has planted a seed. He's "heard" her, and now it's her turn to be patient and give the seed time to grow, which she does. Later in the week, she approaches Daniel again, this time using an "I statement" and the skill of "tell me more."

"Dan," Stephanie says, "remember we talked about my need for reassurance around the horseback riding at camp? I guess I'm still feeling a little anxious about it. Can you tell me more about how it actually works?"

Daniel speaks with exaggerated patience: "Mom, I said it'll be fine."

Stephanie obligingly acknowledges his position in her response. "I know," she says. "I'm sure it will be. And I need to know more about it so that I'm not nervous. I would like you to describe how the process works once you're at camp. I have release forms I need to sign, and I can't do that comfortably unless I feel reassured."

> Connect sentences with the word *and* instead of *but* so as not to negate what you've already said.

Stephanie's artful insertion of a limit—"I have release forms I need to sign, and I can't do that comfortably unless I feel reassured."—is not lost on Daniel.

"OK, Mom," he says with a long-suffering air. He then explains to her how the counselors determine what riding level in which to place the individual campers.

Hearing his explanation does a lot to dispel Steph's anxiety, and she "acknowledges effort" by saying: "I know it can feel annoying when you think I'm being overprotective, and I appreciate your taking the time and trouble to explain it to me carefully. I'll sign the release forms now."

This story ends happily. Stephanie later hears from the horseback-riding counselor that Daniel accurately assessed his level as a beginner.

While he rode with enthusiasm and confidence, he did not exceed his abilities in any way.

> **Seeds that are planted and appropriately
> nurtured rarely wither and die.**

SETTING LIMITS WITHOUT ROBBING OUR CHILDREN OF COURAGE

Dahlia speaks up, shaking her head: "I have such a hard time with letting go. I'm so much better at using the cooperative communication and lifting my kids' spirits when they're discouraged. You know, Caley is just like Daniel. She's so 'out there'—like with the whole belly-button thing. And my first reaction is always to explode.

"I need a 'pause button.' If I could just keep my mouth shut for a millisecond, I'd be able to ask myself whether my communication was going to build a relationship with Caley. But I just have such a short fuse when it comes to the whole independence thing. And sometimes it works to go back and apologize, but I have a feeling that if Caley senses a pattern where I explode, apologize, explode, apologize, over and over again, it's going to deteriorate our relationship."

I once had a professor—Dr. Garry Landreth—who said, "It's not what you do or say; it's what you do or say *after* what you've already done or said." I love that philosophy. It recognizes that, as parents, we make mistakes and that those mistakes are redeemable. In fact, that's why I have my 70-30 rule!

But as Dahlia so astutely pointed out, if she has a pattern of explode/apologize, she may have flipped the 70-30 rule: she's exploding 70 percent of the time instead of only 30 percent. And that's not going to be good for her relationship with Caley. Not only does it "shake the chrysalis," but also it creates mistrust between the two of them.

When a parent apologizes, it has to be sincere. An apology implies "I'll do better next time," indicating that you're working on change. But if next time after next time goes by, and your child doesn't witness a change, she'll lose faith and stop trusting you. Obviously, that's bad for your relationship, but it also disempowers you as a parent. She learns that you don't actually mean what you say.

As a parent, you do need a "pause button" that will allow you to break out of the cycle of explode/apologize. Fortunately, you already know a technique that will serve you here.

Activating Your "Pause Button"

The "pause button" to which I refer is family meetings. When your child demonstrates that she may be going too far in her bid for independence, simply say, "Sounds important. Let's bring it up at the next family meeting." This tactic allows for you to vent your feelings in the meantime to a spouse or friend and ultimately to approach the situation in a measured and thoughtful way.

To maximize your efforts, keep this simple concept in mind: there is a difference between the things in life that are urgent and the things that are important.

Something is urgent when it requires immediate and swift attention. If your child falls off his bike, hits his head, and blacks out, it's an emergency. It's *urgent* that you get him to the hospital and have him checked out.

Things that are important require our attention, but not necessarily immediately. The issue of a belly-button piercing was *important* for Dahlia to address. Likewise, it was *important* for Gary in Chapter 6 to garner information on his children's computer use. In short, most of the issues and situations that we dissect throughout this book can be identified as important but not urgent, because they do not call for emergency response.

One reason that we have trouble employing our "pause button" and using family meetings is that we confuse circumstances that are urgent with those that are important. When we respond to important issues as if they were emergencies, it often triggers intense feelings of fear or anger within us.

Those acute feelings serve an actual purpose if something demands emergency attention, because accompanying them is a surge of adrenaline that allows us to spring into action. If your child needs urgent medical care, that surge of adrenaline will sharpen your mind and impel you to think and act quickly.

> To "press your pause button," all you have to do is memorize one line: "Sounds important. Let's bring it up at a family meeting."

You can probably see how the adrenaline that accompanies those feelings ends up muddying the waters when something is "only" important. In fact, the "explosive" reaction that could save your child's life in an emergency is one that will generate mistrust and resentment if it's prevalent in your everyday relationship.

Setting Limits

When your child is only talking about putting himself in a risky situation, as opposed to actually engaging in a risk-filled act, it's clearly important to address the issue in a measured and thoughtful manner, as we've established. However, what happens when your middle schooler's "out-there" behavior causes him to actually take a risk? For example, let's say you find out that your son drank beer at his friend's house. As unlikely as this occurrence may sound, Focus Adolescent Services states that according to national studies, the most common age for alcohol use to begin is eleven for boys and thirteen for girls! Thus, we would do well to ask ourselves: If something like this arises, how do we set a limit without diminishing our child's self-esteem?

Using Tagged "I Statements." One remedy is to use an "I statement" and tag it with a limit or consequence, as outlined in Chapter 5. In a way, Stephanie did this with Daniel when she told him she had release forms to sign and couldn't feel comfortable unless he would describe the process of riding-lesson placement at camp. Framed more formally as an "I statement" tagged with a limit, it would sound like this:

["**I statement**"] "I'm uncomfortable not knowing exactly how the riding lessons work. [**Limit**] Either describe them to my satisfaction or I won't sign the release forms."

Let's see how it might work if a child comes home tipsy after experimenting with alcohol:

["**I statement**"] "I feel worried and distressed that you're experimenting with alcohol. It's dangerous and unlawful. [**Consequence**] You may not go to a friend's house again unless I can determine that there's appropriate adult supervision."

> When tagging "I statements" with either limits
> or consequences, remember:
> ◄ **Don't block communication by giving
> advice or lecturing.**
> ◄ **Don't use too many words. Short and
> simple is more effective.**

Using the Trust Contract. Another option is to utilize the trust contract introduced in Chapter 3. That might sound like this:

"I'm very concerned that you're experimenting with alcohol. I've trusted you to behave responsibly when you're not under my direct supervision, and you've broken that trust. You'll have to earn it back. You may not go to a friend's house at all for a week. After that, I'm going to call and speak to the parents to make sure there will be adult supervision. If that goes well, then I'll trust you to tell me that adult supervision is present, but I'll check up on you by phoning the parents after you've been there. In a month, if I can determine that you're behaving responsibly, you will have earned back my trust, and you can be unsupervised again."

This example begins with an "I statement" and a straightforward comment about how trust was broken. It gives a consequence of no contact with friends for a week and then sets up a logically related way for the child to earn back trust within a reasonable time.

Should you have to use a trust contract with a child who pushes beyond the limits, be sure to "acknowledge effort" along the way. In the preceding example, it might sound like this: "I hear you behaved responsibly at Sally's house. You're well on your way to earning back my trust."

If your child breaks the contract during the time allotment, you have to let her know that she will now incur a longer consequence. You might say: "I feel disappointed that you broke our contract. It will take you longer to earn back my trust now." You would then increase the amount of time during which she has to be supervised by a set amount.

When to Set Limits. Tagged "I statements" as well as trust contracts are most effective if they're presented privately. To bring up transgressions at a family meeting (unless you have only one child) risks causing your middle schooler to feel judged in front of his siblings. This will "shake the chrysalis" and likely result in embarrassment and shame. Those feelings may engender the perception that he needs to save face in front of his sibs by acting defiantly. In other words, you may get the exact opposite of what you want by presenting transgressions in front of the family.

Ultimately, the lesson for parents is that by putting your relationship at the center of all you do with your middle schooler, you are more likely to retain influence over your child during these as well as the high school years.

9

Talking About Sex, Drugs, and Alcohol

"Can we talk about sex?" Isabelle looks pale. "I'm really upset. I went into Mitchell's room yesterday after he'd gone to school, and there was a condom on his bedside table." Her voice shaking, she continues: "My God, he's only in eighth grade! We haven't even talked about sex yet. All my friends said you could wait until high school to discuss it. Is he having sex?" Her eyes are wide and frightened.

"Let me ask you two questions," I say gently. "First, was the condom wrapped or unwrapped? Second, has he been hanging out with anyone in particular lately?"

"I . . . um," she stammers, "well, it was wrapped, and I don't think he has a girlfriend, but I don't know for sure."

To answer Isabelle's question is tough without addressing it to Mitchell directly. We can make a guess, of course, because if he doesn't appear to be hanging out with someone exclusively, and the condom that Isabelle found was still wrapped, it's likely that he's only thinking or talking about sex, rather than engaging in it. That being said, Isabelle shouldn't wipe the sweat from her brow with relief and avoid talking to Mitchell about the condom and about sex in general. He definitely already has some information (hence the condom), but we all, Isabelle included, need to make sure that information about sex comes to our children directly from us, not just from outside sources.

OUR CHILDREN ALREADY KNOW A LOT

It's a cinch our children know far more than that for which we give them credit, due in large part to the media and marketing. Today, children aged eight to fourteen are a hot target for companies that are bombarding them with sexual images to get them to purchase clothing, toys, and many other products. According to CBC News, "the industry" calls this marketing tactic "age compression," which means "pushing adult products and teen attitude on younger and younger kids." Because of the highly sexualized culture within which we live, most children have heard about sex in some form at an early age—often from their peers on the playground. In an article written for the NYU Child Study Center, Fred Kaeser, Ed.D., admits, "I've been involved in public school sex education for over twenty years, yet I am amazed at the significant numbers of children who express sexualized behaviors at younger and younger ages."

Furthermore, Dr. Charles Schaefer, in his book *How to Talk to Your Kids About Really Important Things: Specific Questions and Answers and Useful Things to Say*, states that if we haven't talked to our children about sex by the time they're seven, they've already heard about it and are probably misinformed.

You may be thinking: "You're *kidding* me! Why should we tell kids about sex even earlier than middle school? They don't need to know before then! Why ruin their innocence?"

Remember from our discussion about the Internet, in Chapter 6, that keeping our kids safe from online predators involves informing them about the ways adults can take advantage of them. You may have assumed that if your child isn't yet using the Internet, it isn't necessary to divulge this unpleasant information.

Unfortunately, keeping our children safe from predators extends far beyond their use of the Internet. Statistics show that approximately one in six girls and one in ten boys will be sexually molested by age eighteen. As if that weren't disturbing enough, the most common age at which molestation begins is three.

Where middle schoolers are involved, we're talking about keeping our children safe not only from predation but also from pregnancy and STDs (sexually transmitted diseases—also called STIs, or sexually transmitted infections), because sexual awakening and experimentation are undeniable facts in the middle school population today.

In an article entitled "Casual Sex Becomes Subject for Middle Schoolers," Marsha Low asserts, "About 50 percent of the nation's teens have had sexual intercourse, nearly 10 percent by age thirteen." Low does not differentiate between those for whom intercourse was a choice and those on whom it was forced. Nor does the survey from which the data come differentiate between oral sex and sex involving penetration. Nevertheless, whether it's being experienced, bantered around, or just thought about, our middle schoolers are aware of sex, and it's the job of parents to ensure that they remain informed of the facts, both to keep them safe and to help them develop a healthy sexual identity.

CAN'T I GET MY SPOUSE TO TELL THE KIDS?

Carol, mother to Tracy, age eleven, and Josh, who's nine, vehemently protests: "I can't do this, Julie. I'm *so* embarrassed. I honestly, really, and *truly* don't think I have it in me." She continues, "I mean, I hear it's important, and I agree, but can't I just get my husband to tell them about it?"

As uncomfortable as we may be, it's crucial that we take whatever steps are necessary to overcome our embarrassment and communicate with our children about this important topic. Fred Kaeser offers this perspective: "Poor parent-child communication only hinders the child's ability to understand sexual matters. The good news is that when parents do communicate well, the results can be profound. In families where effective communication occurs, research shows children are less likely to experience intercourse, pregnancy, and sexually transmitted disease."

IRONY, THY NAME IS SEX

I find it fascinating that during parenthood, we may face myriad situations in which we have to keep our children safe, and we don't hesitate to do so, even if it's embarrassing. If a toddler gets lost in the grocery store, even the shyest parent immediately seeks out the store manager to have an announcement made over the PA system. The mother doesn't think to herself: "Oh, my gosh, that's embarrassing. I don't like asking for favors. What will the manager think?" No, she marches straight to the front of the store. If there's a line, she elbows her way through. No being polite, no waiting a turn, no hesitation. All of us seek to do what's right and necessary for our children's safety, no matter the cost to our feelings or demeanor.

Yet when sex is concerned, parents often want to bury their heads in the sand, hoping that either the topic won't come up or, even better, someone else will tell the child about it, so they won't have to do it.

Passing the job off to a spouse, or even to a professional educator, doesn't solve the problem, however. Not only do our children need to hear the words from our mouths, but also they need to feel comfortable talking about the information with (or at least hearing it from) a parent of the opposite sex. Think of it this way: do you really want your child's first conversation about the facts of life with a member of the opposite sex to be in the backseat of a car as clothes are being stripped off? Of course not. We have to create a foundation of solid values and a healthy sexual attitude for our middle schoolers in the home—hopefully before they begin to experiment sexually with their peers.

"But, what do I say?" parents want to know. The interesting thing is that throughout our children's lifetimes, they ask us questions regarding subjects about which we know very little: "Why is the sky blue?"; "What makes the waves in the ocean?"; "How come Johnny has brown hair and I have yellow hair?" As children get older, the questions may become more academic: "How do you divide fractions?"; "Where do penguins live?"; "What's the capital of Afghanistan?"—and we answer them. We may have a paucity of knowledge about the field of mathematics, natural science, or geography, but we still answer our children to the best of our ability, or we offer to look it up with our child.

Isn't it ironic that during our child's lifetime, we answer literally thousands of questions about areas in which we have minimal knowledge, yet when it comes to sex, an area in which we are very knowledgeable, we find it excruciating to share that knowledge? We stammer, stutter, blush, and squirm, giving our children the impression that sex is unspeakable, embarrassing, and, at the worst, *unnatural*. Moreover, we convey that we are unapproachable on the topic, depriving them of their greatest resource for safety, information, and communication about values—their parents.

HANDLING YOUR EMBARRASSMENT

To help our children develop in a sexually healthy way, we first have to rid ourselves of our embarrassment. To do this, it's advisable to familiarize yourself with and desensitize yourself to the terminology you will need to satisfactorily discuss sex with your middle schooler. Peruse the following list, and ask yourself how comfortable you could be saying each of these words to your child. Rate yourself on a scale of 1 to 10, with 1 being the least comfortable and 10 being the most.

Breasts	Ejaculation	Erection	Homosexuality
Intercourse	Masturbation	Nipples	Oral sex
Penis	Sperm	Testicles	Uterus
Vagina	Wet dream		

If you found it difficult to say certain words, practice saying them aloud and putting them in context. For example: "You don't have to tell me whether you've had a wet dream, but I want you to know that they're normal for boys your age, so I don't want you to be surprised if it happens to you." Or: "Breast buds are part of your developmental process, so if your breasts feel hard as they develop, that's normal."

Individual parents tend to recoil from different types of words. Some parents tell me they're more comfortable with words that have to do with their same gender. For instance, females are often more at ease saying *breasts* than *penis*, and men might be more relaxed saying *penis* than *vagina*.

Parents of both genders report some reluctance using the words that describe function rather than body parts. So, *masturbation*, *wet dreams*, or *ejaculation* may be more off-putting than *nipples*, *scrotum*, or *pubic hair*. It's important for each of us to identify the words that present the most trouble so that we can desensitize ourselves to them, in order to effectively talk with our preteens. After all, how can we even begin to communicate our values about sexual behavior to our children if we shrink from discussing the mechanics of the act?

Finally, remember that it's OK to honestly voice your feelings to your middle schooler. If you're embarrassed, it's OK to say, "I'm a little bit uncomfortable talking about this, actually, but it's important for us to be able to communicate about everything, so I'm going to do my best."

HOW TO BEGIN

With middle schoolers, it's best to find out what they already know before launching into a lecture. If you're squeamish, remember the technique of scripting. Having already written out what you want to say—or just composed it in your head—can be comforting. You might begin this way: "I want to talk to you about sex, but I certainly don't want to repeat information you might already have. Why don't you tell me what you know, and I'll fill in any gaps."

> Use scripting and "tell me more"
> as a way to begin talking about sex with
> your middle schooler.

Isabelle speaks up: "I don't think that's going to work so well with Mitchell." She shakes her head worriedly. "You know that our relationship has been a bit rocky. I think he'll just clam up or walk away."

"I understand," I tell her, "but because you found a condom in his room, you can use that as a conversation starter."

Isabelle looks alarmed, but I continue: "Hear me out. You have to remember that middle schoolers are excellent at being sneaky. If Mitchell hadn't wanted you to find that condom, rest assured you would not have found it. Leaving it on his bedside table so blatantly says to me that he wants to have a conversation with you about sex and protection but doesn't know how to begin. Whenever we find something that has so obviously been left out for us to see, we shouldn't just ignore it. It could be something having to do with sex, like Mitchell's condom, but it could also be an item related to drug or alcohol use, such as a joint or an empty beer can. It could even be a Facebook page that your child 'forgot' to close, or a diary left open on the bed."

Now, just because I've said you can look at a diary that your child "forgot" to close, don't assume I mean you are allowed to search through your child's belongings to find the diary and then open and read it. Middle schoolers deserve privacy unless trust has been breached. That being said, leaving a print item in plain sight and open to a particular page may be a way for an embarrassed preteen to broach a difficult subject and begin a conversation with you. If you do find an open diary or the like, it's your mission to tell your child: "I couldn't help noticing that you left your diary open on the bed. I wasn't deliberately invading your privacy, but I did see that you wrote about _____ . Tell me more about that."

Note that the comment just quoted is a "sandwich." The statement "I wasn't deliberately invading your privacy" constitutes the first piece of "bread." The follow-up "I did see that you wrote about _____ " is the "meat." And "tell me more" represents the final piece of "bread."

Let's see how Isabelle might use the sandwich technique to open her conversation with Mitchell. Here's one possibility: "Mitchell, I found a condom on your nightstand. I'm glad to see you know something about safety. I want to talk to you about sex to make sure you have all the facts you need. Would now be a good time?"

Most middle schoolers will be shocked or embarrassed that their parent is bringing up this topic, and the typical response to "Would now be a good time to talk about it" is a resounding "No!"

If your middle schooler is very resistant to discussing sex (or any other potentially uncomfortable topic), you might say: "I know it's uncomfortable to talk about. Part of my job as your parent is to ensure that you have all the facts that will keep you safe, so we have to have this conversation. You don't have to talk; you can just listen. Tell me whether now or after dinner is the best time for you to listen to me."

> **Acknowledge uncomfortable feelings by "listening with heart," and offer a choice about the timing if your child is resistant to communicating about sex or other uncomfortable topics.**

When you offer a choice about the timing of your talk, it's better to present two options within the same day. If you were to say, "Would you like to listen now or this weekend," for example, I can almost guarantee that either you will forget or your middle schooler will become incredibly busy and you won't be able to catch him once the weekend arrives!

Once you're set to have the conversation, you should anticipate what you're going to actually say.

WHAT INFORMATION DO WE NEED TO IMPART?

Communication about sex encompasses three basic categories: presenting the facts; offering reassurance that your child's development, thoughts, and feelings are normal; and articulating your values.

Giving Your Child the Facts

The myriad facts pertaining to sex range from the basic names of body parts, which your middle schooler no doubt already knows, to insight on STDs and birth control. This section itemizes the areas that I've found most important to discuss with this age-group. For a more comprehensive background, you might want to read Deborah Roffman's book *Sex and Sensibility: The Thinking Parent's Guide to Talking Sense About Sex.*

◄ **What goes where and how.** This category includes the functions of penises, erections, and vaginas. It also calls for related information on the uterus and ovaries, the testicles and sperm, and how it all comes together to make a baby.

◄ **What "sex" encompasses.** Be clear that everything from kissing to penetration is sexual behavior. Both fondling and oral sex qualify. While there's only one way to get pregnant, there are numerous ways to "have sex." When you broach this with your middle schooler, you must not use euphemisms or act shy. Much of the experimentation in which children of this age participate will not result in penetration, so strive to be precise about the other "types" of sex in which they can engage. You will also need to incorporate masturbation, wet dreams, and orgasms into your discussion.

◄ **Birth control and prevention of disease.** It's time to brush up on your knowledge of STDs. This is a territory in which even adults get confused, so you can imagine how bewildering it must be for a middle schooler traversing the terrain for the first time. A central point to make is that STDs are transmitted not only by the penis penetrating the vagina but by oral and anal sex as well. Most preteens and teenagers think that they're having "safe sex" if they're engaging in oral sex. Ask them if they're using a condom or a dental dam, though, and they'll look at you as if you have three heads. (Be honest: do *you* even know what a dental dam is? I didn't until my daughter, then in high school, brought one home and explained it to me! So, just FYI: a dental dam is a thin piece of latex that's placed over the vulva during oral sex to prevent the transmission of HIV from mouth to vagina or vice versa.) The number one message to get across here is that *sex isn't safe just because it doesn't make a baby.*

Factual information can be imparted either in the context of a family meeting or privately. The preferred forum depends on your individual child's temperament. Remember that you know her best, and choose the environment within which you think she will most readily receive the input. Also remember that the information you give your middle schooler needs to be presented over and over again. There's no such thing as "The Big Talk," after which you can slink away and think, "Whew, I'm glad that's over!" Discussing sex and sexuality on a regular basis keeps the channels of communication free of static and provides opportunities for your child to approach you if a problem or question arises.

Reassurance About Normal Development

Reassurance about normal development is rooted in tolerance and respect for the different ways in which children can mature. Some develop more quickly than the norm, and some develop more slowly. Some may gain weight before a growth spurt, while others may be much taller than their classmates for years. Some may experience mood swings; others may not. Some children may find themselves sexually attracted to girls; some to boys.

If your son or daughter feels sexually attracted to a member of the same sex, it's imperative to offer reassurance that this attraction is normal. Even more important in such cases is to reassure our children that we love them for who they are. While the jury's still out on whether children are genetically hardwired as gay, lesbian, bisexual, or transsexual (what Deborah Roffman calls GLBT), Roffman reports, "There is compelling historical and anthropological evidence that these . . . individuals have existed throughout all of history and among hundreds of cultures throughout the world."

You do not experience your own sexual orientation as a choice, but as an integral part of who you are. The same is true for your child. In this regard, remember that the very foundation of our children's self-worth is our unconditional love and acceptance.

The world is challenging enough for our children, whether they are heterosexual or GLBT. We can make it easier for them if we love and accept them and provide a safe, nurturing environment where they can be who they really are.

Here I want to emphasize that accepting your child does not mean accepting irresponsible behavior. To that end, it's our responsibility to communicate more than facts and reassurance to our children. We must also communicate our values so that they have guidelines for the choices they will make as they grow.

Articulating Values

Articulating our values means providing a lens through which we can help our children see and interpret the various sexual messages they receive in today's society. It also means putting the facts that we give to our middle schoolers in a context that reflects our individual belief system.

Among the values that are important for you to discuss with your middle schooler are those relating to sex before marriage, casual sex, and the role of love and trust in a sexual relationship. When we communicate these values (and each family's values may differ), we must remember to engage the qualities of a relationship approach. This means respecting that our child is developing as a sexual individual and also supporting the development of his healthy sexual attitudes and behaviors. It means recognizing that both you and your child have needs and collaborating with your child to make sure everyone's needs are met.

Hint: Your values will be the "meat" when you're using the sandwich technique.

When Your Values Are in Opposition

Here's where things get more complicated. Having just espoused accepting our children for who they are as sexual beings, I'm faced with trying to answer the question: What about people who belong to a religion whose system of values deems GLBT orientation inappropriate? How do we reconcile acceptance of sexual orientation with a religious value system that condemns anything but heterosexual or abstinent behavior?

I couldn't find a way to write this book without addressing this sticky topic, and believe me, I tried! Ultimately, I came to the realization that to ignore an entire population who would be stuck in a position of transmitting values that seem irreconcilable with acceptance of a GLBT child would not only be unfair but also reflect religious intolerance on my part.

I want to reassert that it's in your child's best interests for you to love him unconditionally, regardless of his sexual orientation. To reconcile this fact with one's particular religion that might teach against GLBT behavior leads us to the following question: Can one accept a child's sexual identity and love him for who he is, yet still set limits about his sexual activity based on one's religious beliefs without having the child feel condemned?

Here's my extremely imperfect answer: I don't know. Certainly, we can honor and respect the fact that our child has sexual desires, no matter what her orientation, and still communicate our values about waiting until she's in a serious and responsible relationship before having intercourse. But for a GLBT child, we'd be asking her to deny the fulfillment of her sexual desires for a lifetime.

Can this be done and still keep the child's sense of self-worth intact? Honestly, I don't think so. However, if you're part of a population in which your values preclude same-sex orientation, then here's my best recommendation: at least make an attempt to accept your child's sexual identity, and then separate what he desires from how he acts on those desires. You might communicate to your child that while it's perfectly normal for him to have sexual feelings toward a member of the same sex, or toward both sexes, your religion dictates that he shouldn't act on those feelings.

USING FAMILY MEETINGS TO TALK ABOUT SEX

Respecting our child's sexual development is similar to respecting other developmental needs, using the skills of "listening with heart" and "tell me more." When you talk with your middle schooler about sexuality, the facial expressions and body language you observe will communicate volumes even if the child doesn't utter a word. Acknowledging the feelings you detect and maintaining an open, nonjudgmental attitude in response to any comment will reinforce your relationship. In this way, you build the foundation on which you can stand to communicate facts as well as values.

As it turns out, the most reluctant member of our group, Carol, wound up being the first to initiate a discussion with her children. Here's her story:

Carol speaks with her husband, Andrew, ahead of time, and together they call a special family meeting, saying to the children that they want to discuss an important topic. After the round of compliments, Tracy turns to her mother and asks, "So, Mom, what's all this about? Why do you need to talk to us?"

Taking a deep breath, Carol begins, "Well, I wanted to talk to you guys about sex."

"Oooo, gross," Josh shouts, making gagging sounds. "Do I have to be here?"

His father, Andrew, chimes in: "Yes, actually, Josh, you do. It's your mom's job and mine to make sure you guys are well informed about your growth and development, and that includes the topic of sex."

"But, Mom," Tracy protests, "I already know all this stuff. Can I be excused?"

"I'm sure you already know a lot about it," Carol says agreeably, "and your dad and I are here to fill in any gaps there might be in your knowledge. We definitely don't want to repeat information you already have, so why don't you tell us what you know?"

Tracy sinks down low on the couch, her face reddening. "No, that's OK," she mumbles. "You go."

Listening with heart, Carol acknowledges her feelings. "I know," she says. "It feels super embarrassing, I bet. Even I'm feeling a little awkward. It's really important, though, so Dad and I will give it a whirl, and if you already know something, you can just let us know."

Andrew begins by displaying drawings of the male and female body. He proceeds to point to and name each body part and explain how it relates to sexual behavior. In keeping with the "act as if" principle, Carol looks interested and engaged, despite her own severe discomfort.

**Using books or drawings can "depersonalize"
the material and make it more palatable.**

Both Tracy and Josh exhibit discomfort during the meeting, but neither leaves before it is called to a close.

Carol got off to a good start here! Even though it's likely that Tracy and Josh knew the names of the body parts already, this overture sets the tone for future meetings in which the topics of STDs, oral sex, and the like can be addressed. In addition, Andrew's use of diagrams provides a visual focus for the discussion. Props such as diagrams, books, and illustrations can serve to alleviate some of the potential embarrassment by making the topic seem less personal and more objective.

Now let's see what occurs when a parent has to jump into the deep end rather than wade in slowly as Carol and her crew did.

HOW ISABELLE TALKED TO MITCHELL ABOUT THE CONDOM

Isabelle chose to speak with Mitchell right before bed rather than using a family meeting. This decision was based on her concern that her husband would fly off the handle upon hearing about the condom and derail this key discussion. While I always recommend that parents work as a team for optimal results, the overriding objective is for children to feel that they have at least one parent with whom it's safe to talk about sex and development. If you have reason to believe your spouse can't pull it off, then speak to your child privately. Just be sure that you discuss it with your spouse afterward.

Isabelle sits on Mitch's bed and, using the words we formulated in our group, says gently: "Hey, Mitch. I found a condom on your bedside table. I'm glad to see that you're thinking about being safe. It does bring up the fact that I haven't talked to you about sex yet, though, so I think . . . "

"No, Mom," Mitch growls, turning away from her and drawing the covers over his head. "I already know."

Recognizing his discomfort, Isabelle attempts to listen with heart, saying, "Mitch, I'm clear that you already know, and I see that this is embarrassing for you." She engages reciprocity and acknowledges his need to withdraw as she continues. "You probably wish I would just go away right now. I get that. I need to make sure that I, personally, have given you the information I feel you need to stay safe and healthy." She then offers him a choice: "Would you like me to tell you now, or would you rather wait until tomorrow when you get home from school?"

"Fine," comes a mumble from under the bedclothes. "Fine. Just tell me, OK? Then I can go to sleep."

Isabelle breathes in deeply. Then, talking to the pillow that is now over Mitchell's head, she acknowledges effort, saying, "I appreciate your listening. Thank you." She then continues: "Mitch, it's clear you're beginning to think about sex. Maybe about intercourse, maybe about oral sex—I don't know. I also don't know if you're just thinking about these things or whether you've actually had sex with a girl or with a boy."

Though not her intent, this elicits a reaction from under the pillow. "Mother! Jeez! I'm not *gay*!"

"That's fine," Isabelle says, "but it would also be OK if you were. Even though they represent a smaller portion of our population, people who are same-sex oriented are just as normal as heterosexuals."

The pillow groans. "Do we *really* have to have this talk?"

"Yes, we do," Isabelle says with a calmness that belies how hard her heart is beating. She's encouraged, though, because despite Mitchell's protests, she can tell from the frequency of his responses so far that he's engaged and listening. "You don't have to tell me whether you're thinking about sex or engaging in it; I understand that's private. I do want to make sure that you know you can get HIV and other sexually transmitted diseases from oral sex and from anal sex—not just from putting the penis into the vagina."

The bedclothes become still, and even the sound of Mitchell's breathing seems to cease. The room is enveloped in silence.

Isabelle waits a moment and then says: "Condoms are a good way to stay safe, Mitch, which is why I'm glad that you already have one. You may not know about dental dams, though, which are how you can keep yourself and a girl safe if you're performing cunnilingus—or oral sex—on her."

If Isabelle thought the room was silent before, it's nothing like the wordless shock she can now feel emanating from the bedclothes. Even she feels astonished at the words coming out of her mouth.

Bravely, she stays the course: "I'll get a dental dam so you can see what it looks like. I also want to use a banana to show you how to properly put on a condom and have you practice. Condoms keep you safe only if they're used properly.

"This can't be the only talk we have about this," she adds, "but I wanted to get started. I also want you to know that oral sex and intercourse can be very fulfilling in the context of a committed, consensual relationship, but it's very important to decide if you're really ready for that kind of responsibility by keeping in mind that one of three things can happen if you have sex."

Drawing from the teachings of Deborah Roffman, Isabelle explains: "When you have sex, you will either create a life, lose a life, or change a life. Sometimes, more than just one of these things will happen. So, when you think you're ready, be sure to consider whether you want to risk the possibility of bringing a new life into the world, or contracting a sexually transmitted disease that's life threatening. Also be aware that sex always changes you and your partner. It's the most intimate that you can be with someone, and you have to be prepared for the life change it brings."

Isabelle came a long way from her first shocked reaction when she found the condom. Her conversation with her son reflects both a mature attitude and thorough preparation in the form of scripting and practice. Her investment pays dividends: Isabelle reports that during the course of the next year, Mitchell became more and more open and communicative with her about all aspects of his life, including his sexual development. While he has never revealed the details of any sexual activity in which he might be engaged, based on all that he has shared, she trusts that he is behaving responsibly.

EDUCATING OR CONDONING?

Many parents worry that teaching our children so frankly about safe sex—buying dental dams, demonstrating how to put a condom on a banana—is equivalent to condoning our children's having sex. In counterpoint, research shows that educating our children about sex is the single biggest deterrent to pregnancy and STDs. Citing six sources, Advocates for Youth says, "Evaluations of comprehensive sex education and HIV/STI prevention programs show that they *do not* increase the rates of sexual initiation, *do not* lower the age at which youth initiate sex, and *do not* increase the frequency of sex or the number of sex partners among sexually active youth." In other words, giving our middle schoolers accurate information about sexuality and protection does not condone sexual behavior. In fact, it has the opposite effect.

> Comprehensive sex education does
> *not* equate to condoning promiscuity.

According to the Guttmacher Institute, in the United States, where information about sexuality is not widely available to youths from parents or from educational institutions, "the rate of teenage pregnancy is twice as high as that of England, Wales, or Canada and nine times as high as . . . in the Netherlands and Japan." By and large, parents and schools in the United States have bought into a dangerous "abstinence-only" philosophy when communicating with their children about sexuality. On this subject, the Society for Adolescent Medicine warns, "Abstinence-only programs threaten fundamental human rights to health, information, and life." At best, an abstinence-only policy is ineffective; at worst, it is life threatening.

AND WHAT ABOUT DRUGS AND ALCOHOL?

I've devoted most of this chapter to sex, as opposed to drugs and alcohol, for a couple of reasons. For one, talking about drugs and alcohol with a middle schooler is usually less emotionally intense for parents and therefore requires less "coaching." And two, the principles and techniques are exactly the same as the ones we use when discussing sex. What's different, obviously, is the information that we need to impart.

As I stressed in the guidelines in Chapter 6 regarding computer use, parents need to stay informed about how the outside world may affect our middle schoolers. Awareness without denial is the safest way to raise our children. To that end, lest we believe that alcohol and drugs can't affect a child in the "tender" middle school years, let's open our eyes to a few hard facts.

I mentioned in Chapter 8 that the most common age at which children begin to use alcohol is in the heart of middle school—eleven years for boys and thirteen years for girls. Drugs, too, are cheaper and more readily available in middle schools these days. According to a report by the National Center on Addiction and Drug Abuse written in 2005, "Since 2002, the number of students who attend schools where drugs are used, kept, or sold has jumped . . . 47 percent for middle school students." In 2007, CNN reported that drug dealers are "marketing [a] low-grade heroin to a younger crowd—many of them middle schoolers—[who are] unaware of its potential dangers." Called "cheese heroin," it runs only $2 for a hit and about $10 per gram—well within a typical middle schooler's budget.

Even common household products such as glue, aerosol sprays, or "canned air"— such as that found in the product Dust Off, used to keep computer keyboards clean—can be sniffed or inhaled. These products are particularly dangerous, both because of their easy accessibility and because using such products can result in SSDS, or sudden sniffing death syndrome, in which one "hit" can cause a fatal heart attack with no warning signs.

Because it's critical that we have current information on specific drugs and their availability in order to communicate with our middle schoolers and keep them safe, I recommend that you visit "Parents: The Anti-Drug" at theantidrug.com. You can even sign up for the group's e-mail newsletter to receive up-to-date information and tips for talking to your child.

Keeping our children safe is all about a good foundation of information, a positive relationship, and—most important—frequent, open communication about sex, drugs, and alcohol. As "Parents: The Anti-Drug" says, "Silence isn't golden. It's permission."

10

Sibling Rivalry: A New Level of Competition

"Stop it!" Lidia is screaming at her older brother, Carlos, who is whistling in his bedroom. "I mean it, Carlos: stop it. I can't think. Moooommmmmm! Make him stop!"

Rebeca sighs, slowly pushes herself off the couch where she was trying to read the newspaper, and walks down the hall toward her children's bedrooms. Appearing first at Carlos's door, she says quietly, "Carlos, will you please try to tone down the whistling? Lidia is studying."

Carlos looks up mildly from his computer. "Sure, Mom. Sorry. I didn't realize."

Rebeca then pokes her head into Lidia's room. "Lidia," she says firmly, "Carlos is in his own bedroom, doing his own thing. Just try to ignore him and finish your homework, OK? We're having dinner soon."

"But, Mooommmm," Lidia whines, "I can't concentrate when he does that. And now listen!" Her voice escalates. "He's drumming his fingers on his desk." She shouts, "I'm going to kill you, Carlos! Stop it!"

"You stop it!" Carlos shouts back. "I'm not doing anything."

Rebeca explodes. "That's it! I've had it with both of you. Not another word. Not to each other, not to me. Just finish your homework!" She slams the door to Lidia's bedroom and then walks to Carlos's and closes his door as well.

"Lidia tries my nerves," Rebeca explains. "I use all the techniques with Carlos: no problem. But Lidia is so belligerent. She gets under my skin. I've been trying; I really have. And it's been better since I started working on it. I don't yell at her so much anymore, and I've been trying to respect her developmental level. She's just so much more difficult than Carlos ever was, and so much more . . . I don't know . . . sensitive, I guess. Like she notices Carlos's whistling and the finger tapping. She also gets into these intellectual sparring contests with Carlos because she's so smart. I know she's only twelve, and they're five years apart, but she can hold her own. It drives him nuts, and it drives me nuts. She debates his ideas and challenges what he's learning in school, and it infuriates him."

By way of example, Rebeca relates the dinner-table conversation that took place later that evening:

Things have calmed somewhat, and Rebeca has prepared a nice meal. After a few bites, she asks, "So, Carlos, how's school?"

"Great!" Carlos says. "I just joined the DSC—that's the Democratic Student Coalition—and today we were talking about gay rights. I made the point that our current conflict about gay rights is a lot like what was happening with black rights right before the 1880s and then again in the 1960s . . . "

Lidia jumps in. "It's called the Civil Rights Movement, Carlos, but there are lots of differences. It's not the same at all."

Exasperated, Carlos exclaims, "Lidia! I *know* it was called the Civil Rights Movement." He tries again: "Anyway, I was mainly talking about the 1880s when we first came to this country . . . "

"Gays aren't enslaved like blacks were," Lidia continues, undaunted.

"I'm not talking about their enslavement, Lidia," Carlos says emphatically. "One of the things that moving to the U.S. gave us the freedom to do, for example, was to marry whomever we wanted; we didn't have to be the same religion or background."

"And what, exactly, does marriage have to do with anything?" Lidia retorts, arching an eyebrow.

"It has everything to do with it, Lidia! Gays should have all the same rights that we do, just like blacks or any other minority!"

"So, you're saying they should be able to marry in front of the State?"

"And the Church!" Carlos says.

"No, Carlos," Lidia says condescendingly, "the Church has the right to say what happens in their own religion."

"Aggghhhh!" Carlos pulls at his hair. "Mom! I start out trying to tell you that I made a good point in the DSC and everyone said so; then Lidia comes along and inserts her opinion, and I wind up feeling like a smushed mushroom."

Lidia's eyebrows wiggle, and she declares deviously, "And I am the mushroom smusher!"

I laugh aloud hearing this story, and the group does too. Even Rebeca ventures a smile. "I know," she says. "It's funny. But it's also wearing. They spent so many years getting along peacefully, and I thought I had it made. Why are they fighting like this all of a sudden?"

THE CHANGING RELATIONSHIP

During middle school, sibling rivalry can go one of two ways. Sometimes the situation improves, because your children now have their own lives and are doing their own things, relating to one another only in passing. They may even become close during these years, either seeing themselves as allies against a common enemy (you) or just finding that they have more in common than they thought. On the other hand, sometimes things get worse, as in the case of Lidia and Carlos. Lidia is clearly beginning to blossom intellectually; mix in her intuition that Mom finds her brother easier to manage, throw in a bit of hubris, and you have a recipe for rivalry.

Changing the dynamic between siblings involves discerning the various contributors to the rivalry. Naturally, we don't want to change our own Lidia's burgeoning intellect, and while we might like to change the way in which she communicates her confidence, supporting her self-esteem will be instrumental to her continued success in an academic environment. However, there's one other contributor that we can change, and that's our role in the conflict.

THE LOVE SCOREBOARD: YOUR ROLE IN THE CHAOS

We talked extensively in Chapter 2 about the think-feel-do cycle and how the way we interact with our middle schooler can trigger a cycle for her as well. Add in a sibling, and the complexity of the problem increases exponentially. In addition to an extra think-feel-do cycle, our intervention in sibling rivalry brings up a distinct and unique process that I call the "love scoreboard."

Imagine your children alone in a room together. They are arguing about something. Their attention is focused exclusively on each other and on the topic at hand. You enter the room. Without their turning toward you, or even acknowledging your presence, suddenly the room is a field on which a major-league game is being played—a game of love.

At one end of the field is a scoreboard, across the top of which is written each of your children's names. Under each name is a numerical score that represents how many "love points" that child has scored. Unbeknownst to you, they've been keeping track since they became cognizant that love is a valuable commodity in a family. Each child's goal is to "win" the game—that is, to have the most "love points" at any given time.

"Love points" are assigned—either given or taken away—depending on whose side you, as the parent, take in an argument between siblings. A reprimand (gentle or otherwise) to one sibling in the middle of an argument results in a lower score for that sibling and a higher score for the other.

In Rebeca's story, even the difference between slamming Lidia's door and shutting Carlos's more quietly will result in the acquisition of love points. To reduce sibling rivalry, we have to topple the love scoreboard. There are a couple of ways in which we can do this. The first is by not stepping into the argument to begin with.

Using Nonintervention

Most parents intervene too frequently, believing that the children need help in resolving their differences. The problem here is that early intervention is deprivational in nature. Remember our analogy of the butterfly struggling to free itself from the cocoon? Jumping into the fray when our children are arguing is the equivalent of helping the butterfly out of its cocoon. If we consistently fix our children's relationship problems, they don't have the opportunity to strengthen their own conflict-resolution skills and build their relationship resources. Particularly now that our children are in middle school and their conflicts are less likely to be physical, a more hands-off approach is justified.

> **Children learn conflict-resolution**
> **skills experientially.**

Being in a relationship means compromising on the habits of the other person that irritate us and figuring out ways to resolve the inevitable disagreements that will arise. Living with a sibling is a wonderful opportunity to learn how to live with roommates later on and, ultimately, with a spouse or partner.

Using Late Intervention

Though nonintervention in your children's arguments is preferable, it can be a difficult feat to pull off, particularly if one of your children is asking for your help—or if the chaos is driving you crazy.

When you feel the need to intervene, you may choose "late intervention." Late intervention requires that you draw on the qualities inherent in the relationship approach on which you've been working with your middle schooler: respect, support, reciprocity, and collaboration.

Showing Respect. When our children are arguing, it's easy to view their relationship through our "critical eye" rather than "listening with heart." Sometimes our desire for them to love one another trumps our ability to respect the developmental process of the sibling relationship.

To illustrate, here's a sampling of what some parents in my groups have expressed about their desires for their children's relationship:

- "I want them to love each other."
- "I'd like for them to be able to lean on each other when times are tough."
- "When I'm gone, I want them to have each other to talk to and to problem-solve with."
- "I want them to grow up knowing that their sibling is a treasure—that their relationship with one another is unlike any other relationship they'll ever have and that it is as permanent as their relationship is with their parents."

Believe it or not, these worthy and universal goals are the very ones that cause us to jump into our children's arguments. Then, in trying to force the relationship in the direction we'd like it to go, we inevitably distort rather than support it.

Just as with individuals, relationships have a developmental process. When nurtured and properly supported, they will grow in a healthy direction. Respecting that process involves "listening with heart" if one of your children is asking you to intervene in or complaining about a conflict with a sibling.

Let's see how that might have sounded in Lidia and Carlos's argument about the whistling and finger drumming:

Lidia calls to her mother: "Mom! Carlos is whistling. Make him stop!"

Rebeca puts down her newspaper and approaches her children's rooms, saying as she arrives, "Could both of you come out here for a minute?"

Carlos looks bewildered but complies, while Lidia stays seated at her desk and continues to complain: "Mom! He's whistling again. It's driving me crazy." Upon seeing Carlos, she yells, "Carlos, you're making it impossible for me to study because of your stupid whistling!"

Rebeca recognizes an opportunity here to help Lidia and Carlos develop the important skill of empathy. She "listens with heart" and acknowledges both children's feelings, saying, "Carlos, you look bewildered, and Lidia, you seem irritated."

When we nonjudgmentally validate both of our children's feelings during an argument, we accomplish two purposes. First, we help each child feel understood. This prevents them from needing to escalate their argument to win "love points." Second, we help them learn to tune in to another person's feelings in a relationship.

Many parents try to do this in a different way. A parent might say, "Carlos, can't you see that your whistling is irritating Lidia?" or, "Lidia, look at Carlos: you can tell that he didn't even realize what he was doing." The problem is that this approach ultimately makes it more difficult for us to support the development of a healthy relationship, because it blocks communication. It also results in a redistribution of "love points," which makes the sibling relationship worse rather than better.

Giving Support. We support the development of a healthy sibling relationship when we use the technique of "cooperative communication." After respecting each child's feelings, we can begin "brainstorming." Let's see how this might take form in Rebeca's situation:

Rebeca says, "Can you guys think of a way to work this out?"

"Mom, I didn't even know that I was whistling," Carlos complains. "I can't stop doing something that I don't even know I'm doing in the first place!"

"It's hard to stop doing something when you don't realize you're doing it in the first place," Rebeca empathizes. Then, turning to Lidia, she asks, "Lidia, can you think of a solution that might work, given that Carlos isn't aware of his whistling?"

"He knows he's doing it," Lidia says sullenly.

"I don't!" Carlos protests.

"I guess it feels intentional to you, Lidia. Can you think of a way to remind him about it without yelling? Or, Carlos, is there a way that you might be able to catch yourself or make it more quiet?"

While initially it doesn't seem that a solution is being reached during the brainstorming process, we must keep in mind that our long-term goal is not for resolution of this particular argument. Rather, it's to support the development of our children's relationship skills.

> Set aside your need for a resolution
> to the conflict, and focus instead on supporting
> relationship skill-building.

Encouraging Reciprocity. As we engage in the cooperative communication process, it's helpful to encourage the quality of reciprocity in the sibling relationship. This means helping each child recognize his own needs as well as his sibling's, so that they will be able to eventually communicate with one another more effectively.

In the current example, Lidia needs a quiet environment in which to study. Carlos needs the freedom to express himself in the privacy of his own room. At present, these objectives are in direct conflict. Getting to a place where they can collaborate in order to resolve the conflict, however, means that they must first be able to articulate their desires or goals.

By way of example: my husband is an introvert, while I'm an extrovert. Early in our marriage, the pairing of these two temperamental styles led to inevitable conflict. He would come home from work exhausted from having to interact with people all day, desperately needing some quiet time alone. I, meanwhile, having spent most of the afternoon in an office doing solitary work, needed to "recharge my battery" by talking to and reconnecting with him.

He would walk in the door, and I would immediately begin to tell him about my day. His eyes would glaze over, and I would get angry that he wasn't listening to me. He would feel defensive, and an argument would ensue. Eventually, I'm glad to say, we realized that we each had valid needs that happened to be in direct conflict with one another. That reciprocity was the first step toward compromise.

Along those lines, if Lidia could use reciprocity to communicate with Carlos, it might sound like this: "Carlos, I need a quiet environment in which to study. I know you're not aware that you're whistling. How can we work this out?"

If the communication is initiated by Carlos, he might say: "Lidia, I need the freedom to express myself in the privacy of my own room. I know you need a quiet environment in which to work. How can we work this out?"

It goes without saying that expecting our middle school (or even high school) children to communicate in the manner just described may be unrealistic at the outset. However, simply exposing them to the concept of reciprocity will add value to their future adult relationships. Rebeca can support this process by saying something like: "I hear that Lidia needs for things to be quiet when she studies. Carlos, I hear that you need the freedom to express yourself in your own room. Can you guys think of a way you could work this out?"

When we talk about identifying needs here, we're not referring to someone's simply getting satisfaction. For example, if your children race to the refrigerator to get a soda, and there's only one left, it's an inappropriate use of the word need if one child says, "I need the last soda." Obviously, the child wants that soda, but there's no temperamental, developmental, emotional, psychological, or even physical need present. Therefore, in the second conflict between Lidia and Carlos—the debate at the dinner table—reciprocity applies, but only in the sense that each of them needs to feel respected in a debate. It does not apply to Lidia's wanting the upper hand, for example.

Supporting Collaboration. Recognizing reciprocity leads to the ability to collaborate and compromise. Because my husband and I were able to recognize that we each had a valid need that wasn't being met, we were able to engage in the final part of the cooperative communication process: collaboration.

Over time, we came to an agreement that he would take a less direct route home to give himself an opportunity to unwind. In addition, I agreed to give him ten minutes of breathing space once he arrived—enough time to change his clothes. He agreed that after changing, he would make an effort to connect with me and hear about my day.

As parents, we support collaboration between siblings when we refuse to come up with a solution to the problem for them. This may involve formulating a kind of manifesto by which we resolve to handle sibling conflict. It might take a form something like this:

Parental Manifesto with Regard to Sibling Conflict

- ◄ I will not pay off your argument by assigning love points.
- ◄ I won't get angry at either of you, because that will allow one of you to feel as though you "won."
- ◄ I will not decide how to resolve this for you, because that would deprive you of the opportunity to figure it out yourselves.

Communicating this to our children requires little more than maintaining a firm stance and not allowing ourselves to be dragged into their argument. This may mean offering encouragement and then taking a "parental time-out" and leaving the scene while it still feels chaotic. You could say, "I'm sure you guys will work this out; I'm going back to reading my newspaper."

USING DIFFERENT TECHNIQUES FOR DIFFERENT ARGUMENTS

As you can see from Rebeca's household, sibling interaction and rivalry can take a variety of forms. In the first instance, there seems to be a clash of temperaments: Lidia needs a quiet environment in which to study, and Carlos "whistles while he works," so to speak. In the dinner-table to-do, Lidia's challenge of Carlos could be a struggle for self-esteem. Likewise, it could be about Lidia's wanting power: by playing devil's advocate, she can upset Carlos and thereby feel more powerful in the family.

You could spend time trying to figure out why each argument erupts between your children, but we don't really have to parse them all out and categorize them. The techniques you've learned are fairly fluid when it comes to sibling rivalry, and in general it's OK to pick a technique that feels right to you in the moment. The only reservation is to watch out for the "love scoreboard."

For example, you won't want to employ a technique in a way that communicates favoritism. If Rebeca were to use an "I statement" with Lidia but not with Carlos during one of their arguments, Lidia would lose "love points" to Carlos. That would make the rivalry worse rather than better.

> **Don't run up against the "love scoreboard"
> in trying to tackle sibling conflict.**

Communicating Our Own Needs

It's not just your children who have needs. You have them as well, and failing to recognize and communicate your own needs will only escalate your negative feelings.

The sandwich technique offers a way both to communicate our needs and to handle sibling rivalry. Looking at the dinner-table conversation, Rebeca might say: "I appreciate that both of you are so enthusiastic about history and can speak eloquently about it. I feel frustrated when an argument erupts at the dinner table, because it spoils our family time. I'm sure that the two of you can find a way to discuss this without arguing about it."

The various techniques available for alleviating sibling conflict are rarely mutually exclusive. Thus, Rebeca could also engender reciprocity and engage the technique of brainstorming—before, after, or even instead of the sandwich: "I can see that you both have strong opinions about this. Lidia, I hear that you'd like to have your opinion heard, and Carlos needs to feel respected. How can you work this out?"

> **Techniques are fluid. Be flexible, not rigid.**

She could even use an "I statement" and tag it with a choice: "I would like you both to find a way to discuss this without arguing, or I'll ask you to leave the table so that I can finish my meal in peace."

When you use "I statements" during sibling conflict and tag them with either a choice or a consequence, make sure that the statement is directed to both children. As an example of what not to do, let's say Rebeca directs the following "I statement" to her daughter: "Lidia, I feel annoyed when you argue with Carlos at the dinner table. Either respect his opinion or leave the table." This unilateral remark would result in an assignation of "love points" to Carlos.

If the Conflict Is Physical

The exception to avoiding or delaying intervention applies when one sibling does something egregiously wrong to the other—for example, if the conflict becomes physical. In such circumstances, using "I statements" and consequences to protect the victim is essential. Physical force should *never* be allowed, especially between children old enough to know better, so it's imperative to set firm boundaries and follow up with strict consequences to support the learning process.

What children learn in the sibling relationship is easily translated to their future adult relationships. Because you would never want your child to abuse or be abused by a spouse or partner, you must not sanction abuse in the sibling relationship either.

PROACTIVE PARENTING

"I'd like to really stay on top of this," Sue says. "Maggie and Justin aren't at each other's throats yet, but given that Maggie has started to be so temperamental, I feel as if rivalry might be just around the corner. I can already sense that it's easier for me to be with Justin these days, and I know that it's only a matter of time before she picks up on that—if she hasn't already. Is there a way to proactively address the issue of sibling conflict?"

If you take away only one idea after reading this book, it should be this: proactive is *always* better than reactive.

Family Meetings

One surefire way to proactively parent our children is to be consistent in holding family meetings. These meetings engage all of the qualities that we need to raise our middle schoolers, and they incorporate most, if not all, of the techniques you've learned in this book.

Because they promote family cohesion in a comparatively emotion-neutral zone, they model the excellent relationship skills that siblings need for navigating all of the other relationships in their lives.

By "listening with heart" and encouraging an attitude of "tell me more" during meetings, we help each of our children feel heard and respected in the family environment. This reduces the competitive attitude that can sometimes breed between siblings.

In addition, when we engage one another in the cooperative communication process, we give our children a road map for negotiating their own conflicts—not only with one another but also with all of the other people in their lives.

Articulating Values

As mentioned in Chapter 4, when family meetings are held on a weekly basis, we also have the opportunity to address and articulate our family's values. Sue does this in one of her family meetings.

Sue and her husband, Larry, sit down with Justin and Maggie for their weekly family meeting. After exchanging compliments and then going over old business and any new issues the children want to raise, Sue begins the discussion:

"What I have isn't really an agenda item per se, but it's something I'd like to talk about from time to time in our family meetings." She continues, "I want to talk about our family values—to articulate what we believe in as a family and why we believe what we do."

Maggie looks skeptical and says, "That sounds corny, Mom."

"Maybe it is, a little," Sue responds, "but I'd still like to try it. I have a list of questions, and I thought that when we have a family meeting without a heavy agenda, we could use a little time to look at one of the questions and discuss it. So, the question for today is: What are some of the things we believe in as a family?" She looks from face to face as Justin and Maggie slump lower in their seats.

Larry jumps in: "Well, I think one of the things we believe in as a family has to do with communication. I think in general we believe that good communication is important."

"I agree," Sue says, writing it down in the family meeting notes. "I also think that we believe in respect, which kind-of goes along with good communication. I think we try to communicate in respectful ways with one another."

In spite of himself, Justin is drawn in. "And compromise, Mom," he says, pointing at the list. "Write that down too."

"Great point, Justin," Sue says as she writes. "Compromise is important in a family—actually, in relationships in general. What else?"

Everyone is silent for a moment, thinking (or in Maggie's case, sulking). Then Sue says, "OK, well, we named some really important things that make us who we are as a family. I think it's time for allowances to be distributed, unless anyone has thought of something else we need to discuss?"

The family remains silent, so Larry gets out his wallet and gives both kids their allowance. He asks, "So, how are we closing today?"

At this point, Maggie comes alive. "You said we could go out for ice cream."

"OK, let's go," Sue and Larry say while getting up, and the meeting ends.

Asking Values-Based Questions

The benefit of asking values-based questions during family meetings is twofold. First, it articulates a belief system by which the family either is already living or hopes to live. In articulating our values and asking everyone in the family to contribute ideas about those values, we help our children feel that they play a lead role in the family unit. Even children who fail to participate, as Maggie did in the preceding example, are privy to what other family members say. Knowing that they are included and that their ideas are welcomed even if they fail to express them establishes for children a sense of occupying an important place in the family.

Second, asking for and validating each person's answer or point of view diminishes sibling rivalry. A child who feels heard in the family setting also begins to feel valued. One of the most difficult concepts that our children must understand in their lives is that they can be different from a sibling and still equally valued and loved.

Equal Yet Different

Many times, sibling rivalry erupts because children make the assumption that "different from" means "less than." So, if one of your children is an excellent math student, and another is an excellent writer, rather than valuing their individual strengths, they may think that being different from one's sibling is a weakness. Further, when you compliment one of your children on his strengths, it's likely that the other will feel jealous, even if you had just complimented her only moments before.

One of our goals in the family should be to promote the premise that things can be equal to, yet different from, one another. An easy way to visualize this concept is with money: a dollar bill and four quarters are equal in value, yet they differ in that a dollar bill is made of paper, whereas quarters are made of metal; a dollar is a single unit, whereas the quarters are four units.

When we give our children the opportunity to contribute to creating the values by which the family lives, we give them the opportunity to recognize that they may each make a contribution that's equally valued, even if it's different from what a sibling said.

What Questions Should We Ask?

There are many questions you could ask your family to help articulate your beliefs, and I encourage you to be creative. Some families have "question time" as part of the agenda; others have a different "theme" for each family meeting, such as "Helping Others" or "Kindness." I even know one family who made it into a game that they called "Who Knows Us?" They would begin the "game" with the question, Who knows us? One child might respond, "I do! We're the family that believes in kindness to others." Another might follow, "I do! We're the family that makes sandwiches for homeless people." Every family is different, and you'll want to appeal to your own family's "personality" in setting a format.

To spark your thinking about themes or questions you might pose, here are some suggestions:

- ◄ What does it mean to be a member of a family?
- ◄ How do members of a family support one another's growth?
- ◄ Why is a family different from other communities?

◄ What's beneficial about being a member of a family?

◄ As members of this family, how do we want to treat one another? Why?

◄ How do we want people outside the family to define us?

◄ What kind of mark do we want to leave on the world for future generations to remember us by?

◄ Who are the people we admire whom we'd like to emulate? Why?

As you reflect on these questions, you can see that the answers will begin to define the family as a unit and not just a bunch of individual people who happen to be living together.

Creating a Practical Application for Values-Based Questions

I don't want to leave you with the impression that asking values-based questions is only a theoretical exercise. Articulating answers to these questions can have a powerful practical application as well. Let's see how Adanna used them in her family:

Although Adanna has spoken only about her oldest daughter, Asanti, who's twelve, she has two other children as well: Kiah, age nine, and Manu, age six. During one of their family meetings, she chose to ask the question, "As a members of this family, how do we want to treat one another?" Some of the answers follow:

Manu: "Nice."

Asanti: "With kindness."

Kiah: "Like we love each other."

Asanti: "We want to help one another."

Manu: "We have to share."

Adanna: "I think it's also important to use feeling words when we are angry with each other, because name-calling and four-letter words hurt feelings."

As you can see, each member of the family was capable of contributing to the discussion at his or her particular developmental level.

Adanna did not push anyone to answer more completely or clarify a response. This type of forum allows all of the children to feel that they are making a valid, noncriticized contribution to the family unit.

Later that week, Adanna overhears Asanti and Kiah fighting. Kiah calls Asanti "stupid," and Asanti responds with, "Yeah, well, if I'm so stupid, why are you the one who got a C on your vocabulary test, huh?" Kiah dissolves into tears and runs into her room, slamming the door behind her.

Correctly discerning that this skirmish is important but not urgent (as we discussed in Chapter 8), Adanna chooses nonintervention rather than leaping into the fray, but she makes a mental note to bring this up at the next family meeting.

Two days later, the family sits down at the regularly scheduled time. When they've gone through the other items on the agenda, Adanna says, "I want to talk briefly about the question we discussed during our last family meeting, the one where we answered how we want to treat one another in a family." Referring to her notes, she reads each person's answer. Then she says, "I noticed, during the week, that there was some name-calling—specifically, using the word *stupid*.

"But, Mom," Asanti protests, "Kiah called me stupid first."

"I did not!" Kiah counters.

Rather than becoming absorbed in who did what to whom, Adanna holds up her hand, saying: "I'm bringing this up because in family meeting we said that we wanted to treat one another kindly and use feeling words rather than call people names. So, now we're faced with making a decision: do we change what we said, or do we behave differently so that we can live according to the values we talked about?" Before the children can answer, she continues: "I actually don't want you to answer right now. I want you to think about it first. Let's get through the rest of the meeting, and we'll bring it up at the very end before closing."

Adanna does herself proud here. She appropriately contrasts the values that she and her children had articulated at the previous meeting with how Asanti and Kiah actually behaved. In addition, rather than demand a response right away, she gives them time to think, which allows for a lessening of defensive posturing.

At the end of the meeting, after allowances have been handed out, Adanna asks, "Have you thought about whether we should change what we decided about how we treat one another or if we should try to behave differently?"

Asanti looks down at her hands, and Kiah looks sheepish. "OK, yeah," says Asanti, "I get it." Kiah nods, and Asanti partially turns to her, saying, "Sorry." Kiah responds, " 's OK. Me too."

ONE FINAL TECHNIQUE: LOVE TICKETS

Chapter 1 touted the power of "love tickets" to communicate unconditional love even when our middle schooler is "prickly." Writing love tickets to each of our children reduces sibling rivalry as well: each child feels valued for his or her strengths and loved just by virtue of having been born and existing in our lives.

When love isn't viewed as a commodity to be won or lost, when instead it's recognized as a resource that's freely and abundantly given, then there's no need to compete with one's siblings to get the lion's share. There's enough to go around.

I read about a charming exercise that demonstrates the abundance of love. Each member of the family is given an unlit candle to hold. A parent lights his or her own candle, explaining, "This is my love. Before I knew any of you, I owned all of my love. Then, you came into my life . . . " Here the parent turns to the spouse or partner—or if single, to the eldest child—and continues, "And I was so in love with you that I gave all of my love away to you." The parent lights that person's candle, remarking, "And look! Now you have all of my love, and I still have all of my love to give." The parent then turns to the next eldest and says, "Then you came into my life, and I was so in love with you that I gave you all of my love." The parent lights that person's candle, remarking, "Now look! You have all of my love." The parent turns back to the first person whose candle got lit and says, "And so do you." Then, motioning to his or her own candle, the parent says, "And so do I." This demonstration of the abundance of love is repeated until all family members hold a lit candle.

Writing love tickets to your children reminds them of an indisputable fact: love is an unlimited resource, not to be hoarded and lorded over others. It is not a commodity to be won or lost. As with the flame that lights a candle, it can be given away freely without diminishing the giver or the recipient.

11

How a Relationship Approach Affects Life After Middle School

When my first child was just born, I was ecstatic. I knew I was going to love every minute of being a mother. I daydreamed about holding her contentedly in one arm, chatting with a friend on the phone, with her cooing in the background. I had visions of sitting in the rocking chair, peacefully feeding her. I longed for the day when I could take her out in her stroller and show her off to our neighbors. The final morning of my hospital stay, my heart pounded with excitement. I couldn't wait to leave. My husband helped me pack my bag, we gathered our daughter, and off we went.

When we arrived home, reality hit like a Mack truck going eighty miles per hour, and my fantasies were the casualty. Every time she pooped, it shot up and out of her diaper, covering her back, her hair, her clothes, my clothes. Sleep was nonexistent. She was constantly hungry. My breasts hurt. She cried nonstop. My husband and I were so exhausted that we hallucinated. Life became an unending cycle of bodily functions, laundry, sleepless nights, and equally sleepless days. At one point, I remember thinking in despair, "What have I done?"

On the twenty-ninth day, bleary-eyed and exhausted from having, yet again, been up all night, I heard her cry. I stumbled into her room to feed her for what felt like the 259th time in twenty-four hours. I bent over her crib, and . . .

. . . she smiled at me. She *smiled* at me. She smiled at *me*!

Joy flooded back into my life. That smile erased everything. All the sleepless nights and dirty diapers were worth it.

Now, don't misunderstand me. We had many more colicky nights and poopy diapers. We had the usual dose of ear infections, teething pain, and inexplicable crying. But that smile, and then the way her eyes would light up when we walked into the room, her first steps, her first words, her laughter, all served as an anesthetic for the painful times, propelling us forward as surely as night turns into day.

Middle schoolers are like colicky infants. There will certainly be times when you despair that life will always be this way, that you will always be trying to hug a porcupine with its quills extended. You may feel perpetually challenged to find a way to build a relationship when it seems as though your preteen wants nothing to do with you. There may even be times when you think, "It's not worth it."

But we can take inspiration from what one former middle school "porcupine" said to his mother when he got into high school: "I feel so lucky that you're my mom. You always listen to me. I'm really grateful for our relationship."

You see, unlike with the porcupine, your middle schooler will eventually shed his quills. When he does, it will feel just like the first time he smiled up at you from his bassinet. The colic will be gone, and what will be left is the relationship into which you put so much time.

THE ENJOYABLE ASPECTS OF MIDDLE SCHOOLERS

I recently worked at a soup kitchen with a group of middle school children to make sandwiches and distribute them to homeless people. When there was a lull, the children would be throwing rubber gloves and chasing one another around the serving tables. Then a homeless guest would arrive. Instantly, they were attentive and respectful. They offered coffee and juice in a completely open, guileless manner. They carried on conversations with people less fortunate than they without being stilted or stiff. The contrast between their exuberance and seriousness was delightful.

Looking for and celebrating the enjoyable parts of your middle schooler and then keeping those traits at the forefront of your thinking can be a trial, but it isn't impossible. When the going gets tough, tell yourself that human *being* doesn't equal human *doing*. Who your child is isn't defined by his behavior.

The wonderful children's book *Mama, Do You Love Me?*, by Barbara Joosse, helps illustrate the difference between "being" and "doing." The main character is a little Inuit girl who asks, "Mama, do you love me?" and her mother replies, "Yes, I do, dear one." The little girl then begins a series of questions, asking if she turned into this animal or that animal, would her mama still love her. Her mama replies yes to every question. Finally, the little girls asks whether her mama would still love her if she turned into a fierce polar bear that chased her mama into their tent and made her cry. Her mother replies faithfully, "Yes, because inside that polar bear I would know that you are still you and I love *you*."

Enjoying your middle schooler means looking inside the porcupine and seeing your baby's first smile. It means that when he casually flicks his porcupine tail and you're stuck full of painful quills, you can recognize that it won't always be this way. Just as with a toddler, your middle schooler is in the act of becoming. The metamorphosis may be challenging, but it is not the final stage. Out of the chrysalis will come the butterfly.

FOCUSING ON THE POSITIVE

To tighten your focus on that developing butterfly, ask yourself these questions:

- What is my middle schooler learning?
- What positive things can she now do that she wasn't able to do a year or two ago?
- What are the positive traits he exhibits with his friends? Is he loyal? Humorous? Helpful?

The answers you reach will help you glimpse the butterfly your middle schooler is going to become. The traits and qualities that she exhibits with her friends are likely to be the ones she will show to others in the future, including you. The things that he's working on and learning exemplify his growth; they're indicators that he, and that life, isn't stagnant. He's still in the process of developing.

Appreciating the positive traits of your middle schooler, like my colicky daughter's smile, will serve as a lifeline to get you through the tenuous times. Now, I know it's not always easy to see the soft underbelly of the porcupine, so here's a trick: Late at night, when she's sleeping, go into her room and look at her. Her quills will be tucked in, and you can hark back to the times when she didn't talk back, didn't test you, didn't turn into a "fierce polar bear" and chase you into your room and make you cry. As you watch her sleeping, her chrysalis will become transparent, and you may be able to imagine the developing butterfly within.

IS IT WORTH IT?

When you started reading this book, you encountered the idea of moving away from an approach that gave you control and toward an approach that gives you influence. We've established why it matters that you make this effort. We've observed that when your middle schooler turns into a high schooler, there will be much that you cannot control.

Now let's see how the time you put into creating a strong relationship during middle school will impact your ability to influence your child's decisions and values in high school and beyond. We'll fast-forward and learn how it worked out for some of the parents from previous chapters when they relinquished control in favor of influence once their children became high schoolers.

Jeanne and the Party

Remember Jeanne, the eleven-year-old who wanted a later bedtime and who resented the family meeting? When Jeanne turned seventeen, her mother, Ruth, was called out of town on a business trip. It happened to coincide with a party that Jeanne desperately wanted to attend.

Approaching her father, Jeanne states, "Hey, Dad, just so you know, I'm going to a party tonight, so I probably won't be back until after school tomorrow."

Taken aback, Dave asks, "Why would you not be back until after school? I don't understand."

"Oh," Jeanne says offhandedly, "it doesn't start until 1:00 A.M., so I'll probably just pull an all-nighter and go straight to school."

Dave's first thought when he hears this is to try to seize control and forbid Jeanne to go. Instead, taking a deep breath, he says: "Well, I can't forbid you from going, and I can't control what you do after I go to bed. I am concerned, though, honey. It's really not safe to go out at that hour by yourself. In addition, if you decided you wanted to leave the party and come home before dawn, you would be putting yourself in danger again. I love you so much, and I don't want anything to happen to you. I really hope you decide not to go, but you know I trust you to make a safe decision."

That night, Dave went to bed. In the morning, he went into Jeanne's room and found her safe and sound, having decided against going to the party after all.

Dave and Ruth's commitment to building their relationship with Jeanne in the rocky middle school years served them well. It provided the foundation Dave needed so that he could influence Jeanne instead of vainly attempting to control her. In making this choice, he avoided igniting her rebellion and was able to keep her safe.

Jordan and His Girlfriend

Now we come to Jordan, our overwhelmed slacker from Chapter 2. When Jordan entered high school, he fell hard for a girl one year his senior. They began to date and were still dating at the end of his sophomore and her junior year, when he approached his mother, Olivia.

"Mom?" he says, gaining her full attention. "I have an issue I want to discuss with you. Jessica and I really love each other. And I really want to have sex with her, and she wants to have sex with me. But we're a little afraid of AIDS. How do you get a blood test so we can know we're safe?"

Olivia's heart begins to race. Her first instinct is to blurt out, "You can't have sex; you're too young!" Given, however, that she's put a decade of work into creating the kind of relationship with Jordan in which he feels comfortable enough to come to her in the first place, she doesn't want to blow it now. So, to her credit, she manages to stay calm. Patting the couch where she's sitting, she says, "Well, have a seat, and let's discuss it, OK?"

Jordan sits, and Olivia first answers his direct question: "All one has to do to get a blood test is go to the doctor and request one. If that's what you'd like to do, you can make an appointment with Dr. Peterson. If Jessica doesn't feel comfortable going to her own doctor or talking to her parents about it, she can go to Planned Parenthood, where they'll give her the blood test."

"OK. Thanks, Mom." Jordan seems relieved and begins to stand.

"Could you hang a sec?" she asks. Jordan resettles himself awkwardly, and she continues: "I know how long you and Jessica have been together, Jordan. And I see what a nice relationship you have. I'm concerned that having sex at your age might be a mistake."

Jordan looks slightly distressed. "Why?"

"Well, for one thing, she's a year older than you. Sex is an emotional commitment, and even if you stay together through high school, she will eventually go to college a year ahead of you and will probably want her freedom to date in that new environment. When you've had intercourse with someone, and you get hurt, it's even more painful than just breaking up. I would hate to see you in pain."

"Hmm," Jordan murmurs noncommittally.

Olivia asks, "May I say one more thing?" He nods his assent, so she continues: "You might also change your mind and want to date other girls in your junior or senior year, so Jessica stands a chance of getting hurt too. I think if you can wait until you're older, you won't regret it."

Jordan nods. "OK, Mom, I'll think about it. Can I have Dr. Peterson's number, though?"

Olivia gives Jordan the telephone number. A week goes by, and they're having dinner. Olivia asks, "So, did you call Dr. Peterson?"

Jordan replies nonchalantly, "Naw, I thought about what you said, and I talked to Jessica, and we decided to wait."

Note how nicely Olivia used the techniques she'd learned when Jordan was in middle school. As you can tell, once you have the techniques under your belt, they continue to apply.

RELATIONSHIP EQUALS INFLUENCE

What's remarkable about both of these stories is not only that the teens listened to their parents' concerns but also that they came to their parents in the first place to discuss these things.

This openness is no accident. It is a direct result of shifting from a controlling approach to a relationship approach. All too often, parents spend the middle school years doing the opposite: trying to wrest control out of their children's hands, hoping to stop time so that they can continue to relate to their child as they did during the elementary school years. This is a mistake. For one thing, control is an illusion. We can no more control our children than we can control the movements of the planets. For another, our children will develop with or without us. Choosing to learn the techniques, do the work, and brave the sometimes stormy seas of a relationship approach will help ensure that we walk with our children on their life's journey rather than getting left behind.

The stories about Jeanne and Jordan are only two representations of what parents discover when they commit to learning how to hug a porcupine. Innumerable other stories tell the same true tale: focusing on relationship during the middle school years results in a transmission of your values and allows you to influence your child in positive ways. The techniques will not change who your child is: a child who's an introvert will remain so; a child who prefers to keep some things private won't suddenly be talking about every detail of her day. Nevertheless, the one consistent factor among the children whose parents have embraced these techniques is that they remain in a relationship with their parents, and their parents continue to have influence over their choices in high school and beyond.

MY HOPE FOR YOU

I remember being at the lake with my daughter when she was about eight. As we sat on a blanket, watching people swim and sunbathe, another mother and daughter caught my eye. They, too, were sitting on a blanket. The mother was leaning back on her hands, and the daughter's head was on her mother's shoulder. They were talking in a casual, relaxed way. Occasionally, the daughter would shift to look up into her mother's face, and periodically, the mother would press her lips to her daughter's head. Love shone in their eyes, and their laughter floated through the crowd. What struck me was not just the level of affection between them but also that the daughter was a teenager. I turned to my own daughter and said, "Do you see that mother and daughter?" She looked over at them and nodded. I told her, "I hope that our relationship will be just like that when you're her age." And it was.

That is my wish for you as well—that in learning to hug your porcupine, you create a relationship filled with love, laughter, and affection and that he or she will eventually say, "I'm so lucky to have you."

≡ References

"Alcohol and Teen Drinking." 2007. Focus Adolescent Services. focusas.com/alcohol.html (accessed August 3, 2007).

Anissimov, Michael. 2007. "What Is a MMORPG?" wisegeek.com (accessed July 28, 2007).

"Buying Into Sexy: The Sexing Up of Tweens." 2005. CBC News. Broadcast January 9. cbc.ca (accessed August 5, 2007).

"Computer Role Playing Game." 2007. wikipedia.org (accessed July 28, 2007).

Covey, Stephen. 1989. *The Seven Habits of Highly Effective Families.* New York: Simon and Schuster.

"Cybersafety: Protecting Your Children On-Line." 2007. lcba.com/ benefits/leader/summer07/lcbasummer07.pdf (accessed July 28, 2007).

Darroch, Jacqueline, Jennifer Frost, Susheela Singh, and the Study Team. 2001. "Teenage Sexual and Reproductive Behavior in Developed Countries: Can More Progress Be Made?" Guttmacher Institute. guttmacher.org (accessed August 11, 2007).

"Deadly $2 Heroin Targets Teens." 2007. cnn.com (accessed August 5, 2007).

de Becker, Gavin. 1999. *Protecting the Gift: Keeping Children and Teenagers Safe (and Parents Sane).* New York: Dell Publishing.

Dreikers, Rudolf, and Vicki Stoltz. 1991. *Children: The Challenge: The Classic Work on Improving Parent-Child Relations—Intelligent, Humane, and Eminently Practical.* New York: Plume.

"Effective Sex Education." 2007. Advocates for Youth. advocatesfor youth.org (accessed August 6, 2007).

Elium, Don, and Jeanne Elium. 1994. *Raising a Daughter: Parents and the Awakening of a Healthy Woman.* California: Celestial Arts.

"Emotional and Behavioral Effects, Including Addictive Potential, of Video Games." 2007. Report of the Council on Science and Public Health. ama-assn.org (accessed July 6, 2007).

Euland, Brenda. 1992. "Tell Me More: On the Fine Art of Listening." *Utne Reader*, November/December: 104–109.

Garber, Stephen, Marianne Garber, and Robyn Spizman. N.d. "On Kids and Confidence." World Book, Inc.

"Generation M: Media in the Lives of Eight- to Eighteen-Year-Olds." 2005. Kaiser Family Foundation. kff.org/entmedia/entmedia 030905pkg.cfm (accessed July 27, 2007).

Goldberg, Donna. 2005. *The Organized Student: Teaching Children the Skills for Success in School and Beyond.* New York: Fireside Publishers.

"How Is a Video Game Made?" 2007. answers.com (accessed July 6, 2007).

"IM." 2007. webopedia.com (accessed July 6, 2007).

"Images Kids See on the Screen." 2007. Testimony of Donald L. Shifrin, M.D., F.A.A.P., on behalf of the American Academy of Pediatrics before the Subcommittee on Telecommunications and the Internet of the U.S. House of Representatives

Energy and Commerce Committee. aap.org (accessed August 6, 2007).

Joosse, Barbara. 1991. *Mama, Do You Love Me?* San Francisco: Chronicle Books.

Kaeser, Fred. 2002. "Helping Children Develop Healthy Sexual Behavior and Attitudes." NYU Child Study Center. about ourkids.org (accessed August 5, 2007).

Low, Marsha. 2002. "Casual Sex Becomes Subject for Middle Schoolers." The Body: The Complete HIV/AIDS Resource. thebody .com (accessed August 5, 2007).

"Massively Multiplayer On-Line Role Playing Game." 2007. wikipedia.org (accessed July 6, 2007).

McNeal, James. 2001. Quoted in M. McDonald and M. Lavelle, "Call It 'Kid-fluence.'" *U.S. News & World Report*, July 30: 32. mediafamily.org (accessed July 10, 2007).

Mogel, Wendy. 2001. *The Blessing of a Skinned Knee: Using Jewish Teachings to Raise Self-Reliant Children.* New York: Penguin.

National Center on Addiction and Drug Abuse. 2005. Columbia University. "Schools and Rising Substance Abuse Rates." familyiq .com (accessed August 5, 2007).

"A Parent's Guide to Internet Safety." 2007. fbi.gov (accessed July 10, 2007).

"Parents: The Anti-Drug." 2007. theantidrug.com (accessed August 10, 2007).

Perry, Bradford C. 2001. "The Empowering Inner Potential to End Violence." advocatesforyouth.org/youth/health/assault (accessed September 10, 2007).

Pipher, Mary. 1996. *The Shelter of Each Other: Rebuilding Our Families.* New York: Random House.

Popkin, Michael. 1987. *Active Parenting: Teaching Cooperation, Courage, and Responsibility.* San Francisco: Harper San Francisco.

————. 2002. *Active Parenting Now.* (Revised from *Active Parenting Today.*) Georgia: Active Parenting Publishers.

Robbins, Alexandra. 2006. *The Overachievers: The Secret Lives of Driven Kids.* New York: Hyperion.

Roffman, Deborah. 2001. *Sex and Sensibility: The Thinking Parent's Guide to Talking Sense About Sex.* New York: Da Capo.

Rogers, Carl R. 2003. *Client-Centered Therapy: Its Current Practice, Implications, and Theory.* London: Constable.

Ross, Julie. 1998. *Now What Do I Do? A Guide to Parenting Elementary-Aged Children.* New York: Excalibur Publishing.

Ryan, Michael. 2007. "Is My Child a Target for Internet Predators?" keylogger.bz/is-my-child-a-target-for-internet-predators.htm (accessed July 9, 2007).

Saint-Exupéry, Antoine de. 2000. *The Little Prince.* Translated by R. Howard. Florida: Harcourt.

Schaefer, Charles E. 1994. *How to Talk to Your Kids About Really Important Things: Specific Questions and Answers and Useful Things to Say.* Jossey-Bass Publishers.

"Sleep Drive and Your Internal Body Clock." 2007. National Sleep Foundation. sleepfoundation.org (accessed July 27, 2007).

Society for Adolescent Medicine. 2006. "Abstinence-Only Education Policies and Programs: A Position Paper of the Society for Adolescent Medicine." *Journal of Adolescent Health* 38(1): 83–87. advocatesforyouth.org (accessed August 10, 2007).

Tanner, Lindsey. 2007. "AMA Softens Video-Game Addiction Measure." phys.org (accessed July 27, 2007).

Walsh, David. 2007. "MySpace and Your Kids." mediafamily.org (accessed July 8, 2007).

≡ Index